MW01119518

In Quest of Quiet

A Story of Inner Healing

By David McGuire

1stBooks – rev. 9/6/01

Acknowledgments

I would like to express my love and appreciation to the following people:

To my wife and closest friend of many years, Deidre, whose idea this book really was. Thank you for your continuing support, compassion, and inspiration.

To Julie Innwood, the first to read the book when I thought it was done and the first to improve it in a significant way.

To Patricia Taylor, my long time friend who took the time to take my little book seriously, and whose comments and insights have made it much more than it was.

To the many friends and students, all family by now, who have supported me with enthusiasm and criticism, waiting patiently for my skills to become nearly adequate to the task.

And to Kjell Pettersson, my newly found old Friend in Sweden. Your abilities eclipse my own, and your heartwarming support has blessed me with far more than I expected to receive from this book.

Dedication

This story is dedicated to Swami Rama of Haridwar, whose presence gave meaning to life and love that otherwise would have been undetected by myself and many others.

Contents

CHAPTER   **PAGE**

1   The Forum..1

2   The Handle...13

3   The Trigger 25

4   The Coot and the Glimpse 35

5   The Closet..44

6   Unquestioned Answers 51

7   Happiness and Happiness, Pain and Pain.........68

8   Growing Pains..81

9   Dawn...89

10 Young Pride and Old Confusion.......................95

11 Stretch - Duty into Freedom 118

12 Truth in Passing 152

13 Coming Around 157

Introduction

The world within this book is an uncommon one, but very ordinary. It is not meant to inspire readers with a vision of magnificence as much as to give them hope through a vision of the world exactly as it really can be. Inspiration is lost when experience falls short of expectations, so guessing is a dangerous game. For this reason, everything presented within this book is faithful to the actual life and experience of many people who quietly share the persistence and courage required to make this kind of world their own.

I suppose the idea of quiet will remain an enigma so long as we try to understand it in our usual way. Mental turmoil may be the most common human malady, but it still seems very misunderstood. We all experience it from time to time. The thoughts we most wish to avoid can take on a malignant quality, seeming to build strength from the very effort we put forth to subdue them. This story is offered in the hope that it may inspire others to discover the quiet that flows so easily through some into the lives of those they love.

Those desiring a book of clear facts would do well to look elsewhere. This book seeks Clarity of a different sort. We don't find real Clarity. It finds us. The aim of spiritual practice is to set a stage, open space in a heart, congenial to spiritual unfoldment. Clarity emerges simply when we remove external obstacles we assume are part of our essential nature, but doing this can be daunting until experience permits us to relax.

Until then we're stuck. Without trust we can't relax our grip on the efforts that blind us, and trust is impossible without a glimpse of the Clarity that we cannot reach. In the language of Yoga, truth cannot be seen until our heart eye opens. This happens naturally in the moment when we surrender to Grace, but surrender requires us to abandon powerful habits that we've cultivated to protect what we will come to know as the source of our blindness.

In the end all we can do is practice, but this is enough. Gradually our habits change and little by little we become able to accept grace. The need for courage diminishes as Clarity opens the truth of things to our view, but until fearlessness is complete we need all the help we can get. Inspiration is vital for this.

We can't expect to realize truth through the eyes or path of another, but we can find inspiration in stories shared quietly from depth. And we can avoid a lot of pain and wasted time when we find a track that takes us safely past pitfalls that sometimes seem attractive to our inexperienced eye. I don't believe the track has to be left by a Saint. A few signs left in the right spirit by any quiet explorer who has found a way past a current obstacle is enough for me. This is the spirit that moves me to share this story.

Chapter 1

The Forum

It didn't take Mel long to reach home. She always wa
fast when she was excited, and she didn't have far to go.
paused as her new home emerged from the trees. She was
lucky. It was her first real home, and it was perfect.

Smiling, she skipped onto the front porch and settled into a
large wooden chair that faced the woods. The chair was
wonderfully comfortable to sit in. Her mind wandered through
the house, remembering Marjorie.

Mel smiled as she recalled how they had met. She came
across Marjorie's place on her first exploration of the small
campus. A bright little house nestled in the shade of the trees
lining the campus trail, it touched her with its coziness
immediately. She paused in the quiet of its space. As she stared,
she felt an odd tingling drift under her skin. It was a peaceful
feeling, so she lingered for a while. No one was around to see
how silly she looked, so she just stood smiling and feeling good
for a while. She was surprised when she finally saw someone
sitting quietly in a large wooden chair on the porch.

The woman spoke before Mel could feel embarrassed.
"Hello dear, would you like some tea?"

Mel's smile broadened. "Of course."

"I'm Marjorie. I have quite a few kinds of tea. What would
you like?"

"Anything is fine," Mel said.

"Wonderful. I've just finished making some herb tea I think
you'll enjoy."

1

Mel sat on a large cushion that had been placed carefully on
e porch floor. Slipping out of her sandals, she crossed her legs
nd looked into the woods.

"Here you are, dear. You're welcome to sugar and milk if
you would like." Marjorie was setting a cup of tea and a biscuit
next to the cushion. Mel hadn't heard her coming, but the older
woman's voice had a quality that refused to startle her.

"Thanks. I'm sorry I didn't introduce myself. I'm Mel, and
I have to say this is a wonderful place."

"Thank you. It's been home for a long time. We've
watched the campus grow around us. They've been very kind,
the way they've left the woods. Very wise, too. This always has
been a special place. It would have been a great loss if they had
disturbed it. I expect if you're around you will enjoy it a fair
amount as time passes. Do you plan to move here in the Fall?"

"Yes," Mel said. "I've just signed a contract to teach
psychology beginning in September. Today is my day to look at
the town. I need to find a place to rent near the campus. I don't
need much space, since I don't have many things. Unfortunately
a car is among the many things I don't have, so I want to find a
place within an easy walk of work. I had no idea it would be so
difficult. Rental properties near campus are pretty noisy. I
expect I'm going to get used to a lot of exercise."

"Why don't you buy a place instead of renting?"

Mel smiled. "I don't have much money, and I have a lot of
debts. I had to borrow as much as I could to finance my last
degree."

"Then why don't you just live here? You seem to like the
place, and the place certainly seems to like you. It's time for me
to move on. I've just been staying on until the right person came
along to care for it. Someone moved well by the space. If you
want, I can arrange whatever financing you need. I don't feel I

own the place in the usual sense, but I do have clear title I can pass to whomever I wish."

Mel was stunned. She started to tell Marjorie how much she appreciated her kindness, but stopped short. She knew what would happen if she tried to talk. So she just sat weeping instead, staring into the woods.

The feeling she remembered from standing on the path returned. Yielding to it, she felt herself slip away from the tension that kept her from speaking, but she remained silent. She was watching Marjorie now, enjoying her quiet. It was a peculiar feeling, effortlessly enthusiastic. Mel sensed that Marjorie was happy just to be turning another corner. And she felt the older woman's happiness for her. It was Mel's first real taste of compassion, and she lingered long in its warmth.

Finally she spoke, "Thanks. It will be wonderful to be caretaker here for a while. Leave whatever you wish. It will be waiting for you if you ever need it."

Marjorie smiled, "Let's take a look at the place. Then we can tidy up our agreement and you can move in. If you're comfortable with the idea, there's no point in waiting for all the details to be finished."

By the end of a very busy day, Marjorie was walking lightly down the path with a single suitcase in her hand. Mel had no idea when... if... she would ever see Marjorie again. She had the feeling that an old friend had passed briefly through her life. Mel settled into the wooden chair for the first time. She felt immediately at home.

Drifting back to the present, she thought about what had happened at the forum. So many new faces and friends. Her mind lingered on Jason. She recognized the flush she was feeling. It had been a long time since she'd let herself feel this way. Maybe, finally, she could take time to have a life. It was a pleasant feeling, even with the knot tightening in her stomach. She'd been feeling the knot growing for a couple hours, but knew it couldn't be Jason's fault. It would be normal for her to be a little anxious about finally starting a relationship, and the forum had been extremely stressful.

She thought about the forum. Today had been her first chance to attend. What a day to pick! So much emotion, too much, coming at her from all sides. She couldn't understand why people would subject themselves to such discomfort. They didn't seem to notice the anger that filled the room. Or the fear that had swept in over the anger at the last moment. And then the forum was gone. Just like that. An institution that had lived for more than a century, destroyed because of the feelings of a few people who forgot why they were there.

Her mind wandered to Harold Jacobson. She hadn't met the College Trustees, and she was amazed to see one of them capture the floor shouting, "I think it's time to observe a little protocol!" Watching him struggle to mobilize his dignity against the strain of his yelling, she fought to restrain her laughter.

"I wonder if I look as silly as he does?" she wondered. She knew immediately that she was in trouble. Picturing the two of them struggling to control their faces was more than her composure would allow.

Amazingly, she was saved. Just as her laughter began to surface, the din dissolved into silence. Mel swallowed her voice, stunned. Apparently she was the only one in the room who noticed anything at all odd about Harold's face.

"*Of course*," she thought. "People aren't really seeing him. They're seeing what they're used to seeing when they look at him. What a great article this could make... After I'm tenured. I wonder if he'll ever look dignified to me?"

Mel watched him gradually regain his composure. Finally satisfied, he continued, "I don't think anyone will disagree about certain things. We know cancer of the mind exists, and that it seems to attack all of us. It's obvious that it sometimes doesn't respond well to treatment. But why does this have to be such an issue? Its effects aren't significant if we're intelligent. It's just not a real problem for most people."

A voice strong enough to interrupt him came from the middle of the crowd. "**That's not true**. Our best treatments only address the physical causes of a few problems, and the cancer continues even in the lucky ones who have found some relief.

How can you believe its effects are slight? Don't you see what happens when it overtakes us? Listen to what you're saying. Can't you see how miserable you are?"

Pausing for a moment, the voice lowered. "Look, we're all in this together. Every one of us comes up against the same problem. Sooner or later our thoughts take on a malignant quality, turning our own mind against us. Small uprisings seem to grow until we find ourselves helplessly grasping after them no matter how miserable they make us. And even if we see what's going on, no amount of effort seems to turn it around. We just bury ourselves in our efforts to dig out. I'd rather deal with physical pain than with this. At least physical pain can be controlled."

Harold interrupted loudly, "I would like to move that we submit topic suggestions for all future forums to a full membership vote, and that we stick to a published agenda in all future meetings. Is there a second to this motion?"

The motion quickly was seconded and passed. Then before anyone else could speak Harold said, "I move that this forum be adjourned."

And so it had ended. But at least she had met Jason and the others, and she would see them again tomorrow. With or without Harold and the others, the band of dissenters seemed committed to continue the spirit of open debate that had been the backbone of the forum for so many years. Mel was glad that Jason had invited her to the meeting that would shape the way this could be done.

It was a real mix of people, with secretaries, custodians, and professors bonded by a desire to find a cure for human misery. But why had they called it cancer of the mind?

She remembered asking Jason. He had introduced himself as a member of the Art Department, and seemed to know already who she was.

"Why do you call it cancer of the mind? It seems strange to compare normal psychological turmoil with a deadly disease."

Jason hesitated and yielded to a voice that came from behind her. "Try not to look at it as a psychologist. Just see it as a human being. Sooner or later, our thoughts take on a life of their own, and we get swept to exactly where we really don't want to go. The harder we try to dig out, the more we get buried. There really is a malignant quality to our thoughts at moments like these."

Mel turned as an older and slightly grizzled man joined them. With his baggy pants and loose sweater, he lacked only a pipe to make the stereotype complete. "He has to be a philosophy professor," she said to herself as he relaxed into their company.

Jason's voice tightened a little as he spoke, "Hello, Harley. Mel, this is Harley Sumbridge, Chair of the Philosophy Department. Mel is the new Psychology Professor we've been hearing about. I'm about to invite her to join us tomorrow. I think she'll have a lot to add."

Harley smiled a genuine smile. "I thought that's who you were. I'm sorry to intrude. I just wanted to introduce myself. Jason's right. Quite a few people are talking about you. Your approach is causing quite a stir."

Mel flushed. "I assume you're talking about my class on Analysis. I'm sorry. I'm really not trying to turn the campus into a circus. Some of the kids haven't caught on yet that the field experience is supposed to aim them back at themselves. I think analysts should personally experience the difficulty as well as the success in uncovering what we hide from ourselves. I don't believe analysts can help others until they know from their own experience how we all conceal what troubles us, and I really think they can help others better when they have less to work on themselves. That class is intended to give them the chance to actually experience what keeps us from seeing the root of our feelings."

"That's not a particularly academic approach," Harley said quietly.

"No, I guess it's not. But I'm not trying to teach those kids about analysis. In that class I'm trying to help them become analysts."

"Good." Harley's smile was relaxed, and contrasted with Jason's stiffness.

"That's odd," Mel thought. Then she immediately forgot. Jason was talking, and his voice had a lilt that was absolutely charming.

"The goals you have for your students are essentially the same as the goals of our forum. I'm sure we'll get along very well. It will be a pleasure hearing a fresh voice. We'll be meeting in the Gallery tomorrow at tea time." Bowing gracefully, Jason lifted her hand and kissed it gently.

"See you tomorrow," was all she heard. Then he was gone, after flashing the prettiest smile she had ever seen.

Mel had no idea how much time had passed when she noticed Harley standing, watching. Not staring. Just taking everything in. Mel knew she was blushing, but Harley seemed unthreatening so her composure returned quickly.

Harley spoke first. "Jason really is charming. I enjoy watching when his breeding comes into play. It's something I've never really understood, and I don't guess I ever will. But it certainly is interesting to see. I expect you'll enjoy it too. I know I would if I were you."

"He is awfully pretty," she smiled.

Mel couldn't believe what she was saying. She was a private person, and she was talking this way with a man she had known for less than five minutes. He was older, but it definitely didn't feel like she was talking with her father. It felt more like talking with a college dorm friend.

Harley replied, unaware of her thoughts. "I'm sure there's something behind the hair. I'm just not sure what it is. But that doesn't matter for the moment. Jason brings a lot of energy to the forum, and he has valuable connections. I expect tomorrow's meeting will be very interesting."

Harley shook her hand, and turned to leave. "It's been nice meeting you. I agree with Jason. You should be a refreshing addition to the forum. I'll look forward to seeing you tomorrow. Enjoy your research."

Mel remembered watching him shuffle off. They were so different. It was almost as though they tried to be opposites, but each of them seemed completely dedicated to the forum in their own way. Then, with her mind drifting back to Jason, she went to bed. She was really looking forward to tomorrow. Smiling, she slid quickly into sleep.

The next day passed quickly toward tea time. Mel arrived early, happy for an excuse to see the school's art gallery for the first time. Stepping into the building, she was startled by a chill creeping into her back. "Can't I can go anywhere? Where is this coming from?" She scanned the room. As usual, she found nothing to explain her discomfort.

Turning away from the feeling, Mel moved toward a large atrium. "Might as well see what this place is like," she sighed.

As soon as she arrived, Mel knew she'd made the right move. The atrium passed into a surprisingly large conservatory filled with a collection of plants from around the world. Her body warmed as she entered the moist air. She walked through the lush growth until she found a small pond, settling onto a bench at the water's edge. Snuggling into the seat, Mel knew she had discovered a special place. Then, as her mind quieted, she remembered her dream.

Watching an ocean scene... nothing but beautiful blue water... one small boat... a lifeboat... just one person in it... lanky... familiar somehow... guiding it through the water... people in the water... some are swimming... trying to get in the lifeboat... he's going right by. There's me... drowning... can't swim... just looking at him and going limp... he's grabbing me now... not the others... just me... why not them?

Because they aren't drowning.

But they want in.

Not for the right reason. This is a lifeboat.

You don't have the right to keep them out. Sooner or later they'll drown.

9

My boat only holds a few. Let them swim until it's not a game. Then I'll do what I can.

But they really want in now. They sound so desperate.

Why?

They want in.

Why?

They see me. They deserve to be in as much as I do.

That doesn't matter. You're not here because you're better than they are. You're here because you were drowning.

Where are we going?

Here.

Aren't we here already?

Not quite, but soon we will be. Then you can float without me.

It was such a pleasant voice, vaguely familiar. It faded as Mel began feeling the presence of others. Gradually opening her eyes, she glanced at her watch. Tea time.

"I'll have to come back," she thought as she drifted toward the gallery hall.

The meeting was beginning just as Mel arrived. She moved quickly to a seat in the last row. It soon was clear that Harley and Jason were the most vocal members of the group. "There's a real rivalry between them," she mused. "Jason is more assertive, but people seem to turn to Harley as a leader. It's no wonder. He's so peaceful by comparison. Jason seems driven. This isn't good for somebody who's trying to become a leader in the search for a cure for cancer of the mind. And he knows he's swimming upstream, which isn't helping him."

Mel watched her thoughts gradually disappear into Jason's voice. Her stomach tightened. Jason was cornered.

"It just makes sense to me," he was saying, "that if we go after a grant we should ask them to set aside a wing in the art building for the project research. My father is on the Board of Trustees, and he has guaranteed that we can get as much space here as we want. There's no reason why we have to be spread out over the entire campus."

Harley spoke more quietly, "Perhaps not, but there is a reason why we might *want* to be. It's not clear to me that there's any advantage to a central research facility for a project like this. We might function more capably in our familiar surroundings. Unless experience proves otherwise, I think we should remain in our current offices. If what you say is true, anyone who needs or wants to work here can move in if they wish."

Jason flushed at the general sounds of approval. "Okay," he responded. "Have it your way. I know better than to argue with you when your mind is made up."

Harley didn't take the bait. He just smiled gently and spoke to the crowd. "Then it's agreed that we will pursue the research grant and that we'll plan to retain our current offices and labs. Is there anyone who is uncomfortable with this?"

The general enthusiasm of the group was unambiguous, so Harley continued as he turned back to Jason, "This is the nicest place on campus for meetings, so it would be great if your father could work out a way for us to use it whenever we need to get together. Most of the time we can just use email, but we'll need computers for this. Do you think your father could arrange to set up a computer network as part of the grant?"

Jason's enthusiasm revived, "Absolutely. All I have to do is make it part of the proposal. Let me know exactly what to ask for and I guarantee it'll be there."

Jason was as good as his word. Within a month the project was officially funded. With computers and staff in place for the beginning of the next semester, the project suddenly found itself underway.

Chapter 2

The Handle

The new semester was only a month old, but Mel was becoming comfortable with her new routine. She began each day with a visit to her favorite spot by the little pond. Sitting there was peaceful, and it seemed to allow a quiet feeling to carry her through the day.

This morning was unusually dreary. Clouds had rolled in just as she arrived. They filled the air with drizzle that looked like it would last all day. Under the glass roof was as always, lush and warm. Mel smiled as she recalled why she had first wanted to make these morning visits part of her daily routine. Jason had seemed so important, but she hadn't run into him once. For a while she was disappointed but she soon came to appreciate the solitude she had found instead, especially as tensions rose within the project.

It was hard to tell why, but Harley and Jason seemed to annoy one another more with each passing day. Usually they just kept to themselves, since both of them secretly dreaded their confrontations. Despite this, Mel and the others frequently had to watch as the pair found themselves facing off over one thing or another that suddenly seemed very important. Today was one of those days.

Sitting at his computer, Jason's head bobbed with his pulse as he stared into his screen. The message had just come in, so Harley probably was watching on the other end. He read it again, slowly.

*Why should we legislate method to people whose main value is their creativity? *Harley**

Eventually Jason found his reply.

*I just thought it might be nice if we made a token effort to avoid duplicating mistakes. And it might not be a bad idea to remember that eventually we may have to legitimize our results to others. *Jason**

Within seconds, his screen lit again.

*Okay. *Harley**

Jason pictured Harley's irritating little smile at the other end. It was hard to tell if Harley was needling him on purpose. But even if he wasn't, Harley was very good at concealing whatever fear or anger he might be feeling. This alone was enough to annoy Jason.

Unless specified as private, all posts were sent to the entire network. Since both Harley and Jason seemed to want their confrontation to be public, everyone was forced to endure the squabbles whenever they erupted. Mel read the latest account as she sat for her morning tea. "Another sandbox fight," she sighed. "It's hard to see how we get anything done."

But things *were* getting done. The disease was being watched, and the project was coming alive with fresh ideas. Mel looked at the next message.

*The distress seems to occur most frequently when minds are weak. Shouldn't we simply develop techniques for strengthening the mind? Eventually everyone's mind could be made strong enough to resist wandering. *Jason**

Before she had time to think, Mel's fingers had found her keyboard.

*Better to pursue a positive than a negative cure. *Mel**

"I'll bet he comes back to that one," she said as she finished. She was right.

*It's difficult to see why a positive effort to build positive mental abilities would be seen as negative. *Jason**

Mel smiled and thought for a moment. "Should I leave this one alone? I don't think so. He's not only being sarcastic, he's wrong. And this is important." Taking a deep breath, she typed her response.

*Positive = effective in establishing the right thoughts. Negative = effective in stopping the wrong ones. *Mel**

She was a little surprised at the next message.

*Meeting in gallery at tea time tomorrow. RSVP email regrets only. *Jason**

Mel arrived early enough to sit a while by the pond before the meeting. By tea time, she was feeling rested and ready. "I wish I knew why I was worried," she thought as she walked toward the gallery hall. "I have nothing to lose, and I know I'm right."

As she walked into the room, her body churned warmly. "It must be anger," she thought, "but I've never felt it that way before. That must be it! I've never picked up on anger before without feeling afraid of it. This is going to be interesting."

Moving toward the back of the room, Mel was intercepted by Jason before she reached her usual spot. "Come on up front," he said cheerily. "This involves the two of us, and we really should be where people can hear us."

Mel felt her face become flushed. And she felt something else too, a sharp pain in her stomach. "That's not me," she thought. "That's Jason. For all his bravado, he's scared to death. Why would he want to do this to himself?"

Jason ushered Mel to a chair that definitely was up front. Up on a small stage. "I have less to lose than you do," she said to herself as she turned her chair to face a little toward Jason. Smiling, she sat and pretended she was on her favorite bench. She tried to ignore Jason's trembling knees as he stood to speak.

"Thanks for coming," he began. "We have to make a decision to move decisively in our research, and we finally have an idea that we can pursue directly. By developing techniques for strengthening rationality and mental focus we can move directly toward a cure for cancer of the mind. I believe we should channel all of our energies into developing these techniques, beginning immediately. I've invited Mel to speak on behalf of anyone who might oppose this idea so we can reach an accord and begin to move forward without delay."

Gesturing to Mel, Jason retreated to his chair.

Mel stood slowly, gathering her thoughts. By the time she had reached center stage she was ready. She looked at Jason, who looked away. "You've just removed yourself from the province of my care," she thought as she turned to the audience.

She began slowly, "If I really had been asked to speak on behalf of the people who might oppose this idea, I would have refused. I'm happy to speak for myself, but I don't really know if anyone else shares my feelings. And even if they do, I think it's completely inappropriate for me to speak for others without their consent."

She glanced at Jason before continuing, "On top of this, it's illogical for me to be the one making a case. Jason is the one who wants to make a change, so he should be the one talking. However, since he has requested me to speak, I'll speak. And since he is the only one who has empowered me as a spokesperson, I'll speak on his behalf."

Mel paused, feeling a chill in her back. "I guess that got his attention," she thought. "It doesn't seem like he's in a position to talk right now, so I may as well settle down."

She took a languid breath and then continued. "As a matter of fact I think it's a good idea. Learning how to strengthen rationality and mental focus can't hurt. I'm just uncomfortable assuming that this will attack the real problem. Sooner or later we have to move toward a positive cure, but in the meantime this seems like a good idea."

Mel turned to Jason and gestured for him to speak. The chill in her back had subsided.

Jason smiled. His liquid voice had returned. "Whether or not this moves us to a final cure, I agree whole-heartedly with Mel. We all should focus our efforts immediately on devising techniques for strengthening the mind, and not only with exercises. We need regimens of rest and nutrition that can become part of our personal routine. I move we do so immediately."

The movement was seconded and passed without further debate.

Results came quickly. Many people felt their concentration becoming more focused and sustained. On top of this, people were beginning to get some relief from their mental distress. Mel watched and waited. She had a feeling it wouldn't last long.

The first message came one morning shortly after dawn, just as she was pouring her morning tea.

Rest seems to help, but my intellectual focus doesn't seem to be all that related to my mental turmoil. Mild attacks seem to yield, but strong ones are as bad as ever. Are others having the same experience?

"Unsigned," Mel noticed as she read her screen. "Things will open up now." She was right. Within minutes the floodgates opened.

Definitely. We must have missed something. Maybe our basic ideas about mind, or about the cancer, are wrong. Either way, it seems like a blind alley.

I agree. All of our efforts so far have been spent analyzing and strengthening our ability to concentrate, but some jobs are simply beyond the power of concentration.

"Sooner or later somebody has to sign their message," Mel thought as she began to type.

*Right. When I try to hear a pitch in music, my ability isn't helped by increased effort. In fact, the harder I try, the less I can tell if a note I am singing is flat or sharp. *Mel**

A reply came immediately.

*Interesting. I notice the same thing also when I have difficulty with my writing. The harder I concentrate, the less I can write. *Harley**

"Yes!" Mel hissed excitedly as she typed.

*There certainly seems to be more than just one kind of process that can go on when we're thinking. Creativity must be the key. Maybe creativity has to be strengthened along with our intellectual focus. But this won't be easy. How can we strengthen something that abandons us whenever we exert ourselves to use it? *Mel**

This thought ended the quick exchanges. Several days passed before Mel's next message.

We've been trying to understand creativity the same way we understand intellectual focus. So far all we've found is that it doesn't yield to this kind of study. Sooner or later we have to quit wasting our time. We're going to have to use our creativity to understand itself. *Mel*

She expected a reply from Harley, but Jason answered first.

That's a clever thought, but there's a problem. The funding we receive requires us to do scientific research. Whatever we do, we cannot abandon our rational method of analysis. Otherwise we leave behind more than just our funding. If we allow "creative looks" to support our research we'll abandon any hope of understanding things the way they really are. *Jason*

Mel was stunned.

But why? Our knowledge feels deepest when it's based on more than just intellectual understanding. Many things simply can't be explained, or done, without creativity. *Mel*

She sighed as Jason's words flashed back.

There is a reason why scientific method is objective. *Jason*

Mel slumped into her chair. Pulse pounding, she knew there was no point in trying to respond. Staring at her screen, her heart leapt as it lit again.

Just because scientific method avoids irrationality doesn't mean it also avoids growth. What's the point in science if it doesn't lead to discovery? *Harley*

Mel smiled, imagining Jason watching his screen.

We don't have to be creative in order to find truth. But we do have to be rational and rigorous. It doesn't take creativity to examine evidence, and it doesn't take creativity to evaluate it *against a rational standard. What it takes is rigorous method to determine where we should look and to evaluate what we've seen. We have to be objective, taking a rational look at things we can share publicly and scientifically. That's the point of scientific method. *Jason**

Harley had expected something like this, so he had a response already typed and ready to send. It came immediately.

"Poor Jason," Mel giggled as she read.

But how do we know where to look? And when we finally decide where to look, how do we do so without letting our expectations prejudice what we see? The point is, we have to have creative innocence or we won't really see what's staring us in the face. Rational understanding simply isn't enough. Science is a pursuit of growth in knowledge of the universe, and real growth comes through discovery of meaning that is deeper than any amount of intellectual understanding. Depth unfolds through creative innocence, not intellectual understanding. *Harley*

Time dragged until the next message finally appeared.

Are you saying that we're not supposed to be objective? I doubt if many scientists would agree. *Jason*

Again, Harley's response was ready.

I agree that we have to be objective, but I don't believe you understand what this means. We simply have to bounce our findings off of others so that no one gets swept away by their imagination or incompetence. Scientists do this by having other scientists duplicate their experiments. This is a rational approach. But science depends on doing much more.

We're talking about getting stuck in our research. Scientists get stuck too. Creativity gives us growth. Rationality gives us rigor. We need both, or there is no point to our research. Of *course we have to use scientific method. But scientific method refers to more than analysis. It is a method for discovery, and it can be applied to creative insights as well as to anything else. Insights can be corroborated like anything else, and they are necessary if we want to find what we're looking for. *Harley**

There was no response, but Jason was not finished. For several weeks he carped to anyone who would listen about Harley's "Objective Idealism". Mel was surprised to see his following grow. All the while, Harley did nothing. He seemed to just trust his supporters to defend his views. Mel knew he was waiting, but for what?

Finally it came.

Full meeting in gallery. We have to get this settled. Tea time tomorrow. *Jason*

The meeting didn't last long. Jason mobilized his supporters and prepared to speak, but Harley was watching. Before Jason could begin, Harley rose and said, "This is pointless. Our arguments are merely prolonging an unnecessary debate. This issue doesn't have to be settled in order for us to find what we're really looking for. Why don't we just move on? The important thing is to get to the bottom of things, not to debate how we can get there. We all should just use whatever strengths we have to find a cure."

Jason just watched as a quick vote was taken. It was agreed to move on, and the group enthusiastically dispersed. Mel and Harley left together. She smiled wryly, "We're supposed to be learning how to strengthen and control our creative capacity. Of course nobody knows what this means or how to do it, but at least we're stumbling around together for a change."

The thought stuck with her for the rest of the day and into the night as she drifted into sleep. By morning she had new ideas. She sent her message at her usual hour.

21

We know we can't cure the disease merely by strengthening our intellectual focus. We know the key lies somewhere in our creativity, but we're still grappling with our understanding instead of moving ahead. We don't need to understand our creativity in order to use it. I don't have to understand electricity in order to turn on a light. I just have to find the right switch. After all the work we have done, the harder we try the more we fail. This has been going on long enough. It's really time to look another way. *Mel*

Sipping her tea, Mel noticed her screen lit quickly.

Looking in another direction is the obvious choice when a theory fails, but your statement doesn't help us <u>find</u> the direction. *Jason*

"Of course, Jason. Let everybody know you thought of that a long time ago." Mel set her jaw and typed her reply.

I didn't mean merely to look in another direction. I meant to look in another <u>way</u>. Instead of trying to look <u>at</u> creativity, it might work better to look <u>with</u> it. We don't need to stare at something in order to use it. To learn about creativity all we need to do is allow ourselves to bend with whatever inner movement seems most congenial to clarity. Right now we don't need more answers. What we need most are good questions. *Mel*

There was no reply.

Although Jason seemed to be unaffected by the exchange, her message had a noticeable impact on the rest of the project. Old questions were reformulated and progress was measured in the refinement of questions rather than in the accumulation of answers. And instead of searching for a method to strengthen focus, people began to accept that surrender was somehow central to connecting with their creativity.

Mel's messages had become the center of attention. Whenever the time seemed to be ripe, people gathered around monitors and waited for her next inspiration.

Mel almost always rose early, walking across campus to arrive at her favorite bench before dawn. More and more often she would feel enveloped by warmth as her mind floated through whatever problems had stopped her the evening before. Shortly after dawn on a good morning she would be at her computer sharing her thoughts with the growing number of early risers. Her next message reached almost everyone immediately.

*We've quit trying to stare at creativity directly. Maybe we shouldn't even try to look at it indirectly. We know we don't need to understand it in order to use it. We know that instead of just looking **for** creativity we need to look **with** it. Remember* Flatland. **Mel**

An unusually subdued Jason was the first to reply.

What is Flatland*? *Jason**

Flatland *is a fairly old book about perceptions and knowledge in a two-dimensional universe. Imagine living as a dot on a page. Looking at a line from the end would cause it to look like a dot. It would be impossible to identify a line as a line without moving around it to see how it changed length. And a circle would look like a line, except that it's length would be constant as we moved around it from the side. Someone viewing this two-dimensional world from above would see it differently. With their three-dimensional perspective they would be able to see things, relationships and truths, that were invisible to the two-dimensional inhabitants. Like the inside of a circle.*

I believe creativity is like this. Intellectual understanding lacks a dimension of depth that is normal to the perspective of creativity. In Flatland, *three-dimensional viewers have the power to see themselves and Flatlanders as well, but Flatlanders*

23

cannot see beyond their two-dimensional realm. They just aren't able to see the depth beyond their two-dimensional perceptions.

In the same way, creativity can view the realm of depth and the intellectual world with equal clarity, but our intellectual faculty can only see intellectual objects. It just doesn't have the power to see the depth that is open to creativity.

*There's more, too. If this is true, it means that our creativity can perform both intellectual and creative tasks quite well, even though rational intelligence is only capable of performing intellectual tasks. This says to me that even rational tasks might go better if we could somehow release them to our creative faculty. *Mel**

Mel didn't expect a quick response, so she made herself some tea. When she returned, a message was waiting.

*I think I can see what you mean. But how does this help us find a way in? *Jason**

I don't know. Staring at a sentence certainly doesn't help me understand it. The "aha" experience just comes by itself. Maybe the question that prompts us really is the key. We can control the content of our questions, and they might somehow push us into one mental faculty or the other. One thing is for certain. In the end, we don't "get it" because we chased down the meaning. We "get it" because we let it sink in without resisting it, and the sinking in depends somehow on our creative faculty.

*I think this is true whether creativity gives us knowledge or a work of art. I don't think we really create anything ourselves, but we do have to develop a few skills before we can participate in origin. There has to be a way to encourage this. *Mel**

Chapter 3

The Trigger

Things were beginning to change. The "way of the way" was now the center of attention. Instead of discussing creativity, people were talking about participating in origin.

It hadn't taken long for this to catch on. It started one evening as Mel walked across campus. Following her habit, she mused as she walked alone. "I'm not unfriendly," she said to herself, "just private." She watched as a feeling of loneliness washed over her.

She was happy when someone approached her during one of these moments. They were coming more and more frequently.

Mel turned toward the sound of footsteps behind her. "Hi Jason," she said. She paused for him to catch up. "You look like you're in a bit of a hurry." Mel felt her pulse quicken as he approached.

"I guess so," he heaved. "I was hoping to catch you this evening, but you got here a little earlier than usual."

"I'm sorry. What was it you wanted to talk about?"

Jason paused a moment to catch his breath before he continued, "I was wondering if I could ask you about your email comments. A few of us were talking about them last night at supper, and we can't agree on what you meant."

Mel felt urgency in his voice. "He must have a lot riding on this," she thought.

She tried to hide her concern as she spoke, "You mean about creativity being a *how* instead of an object?"

"Yes, but that's not the way you put it in the email."

"I remember, but that's what I meant. At least I think so. Sometimes words just come out and it takes a while for me to understand what I said. It's almost like someone else was talking. The things that make the most sense seem to come this way though. Maybe it'd help to talk it through a little."

Jason brightened. "Great. There's a difference between saying creativity isn't a thing and saying it isn't even an object. This is helpful. I was still caught in trying to analyze everything, so I guess I missed the point. Instead of trying to look at creativity as a strange new kind of object that has to be analyzed in a new way, the whole point is that it doesn't work if I try to analyze it at all."

"Right," Mel replied. "We have to keep from forgetting why we're searching. In the end all that matters is whether or not we can do it, not whether or not we can talk about it intelligently."

Jason said, "That's exactly what I thought, and you're saying that we can't be creative by trying to be creative. It can't be an object that we aim at directly. I have to connect with my creativity creatively. I can't do it by thinking about it any more than I can create a work of art by thinking about it. I have to yield to the process."

"Right. Otherwise you aren't participating in the origin of a work of art. You're just stuck thinking about it."

Jason beamed back, "So the goal is to participate in origin. That's what creativity really is."

"I guess so," Mel smiled as they reached her home. She noticed a warm feeling as she thanked Jason for his conversation and said good night. For a moment her loneliness was gone.

Time began to pass more quickly, and the atmosphere of the project seemed to lighten as Spring approached. With Jason organizing a nucleus of enthusiasm around Mel, her ideas about origin spread quickly. The two were together much of the time.

"Your ideas come across more effectively when we're actually talking," he said.

Mel had to agree.

Although she found less private time, she still slipped away regularly to sit alone by the pond. Staring into its depth, her mind would become quiet. "The deeper I stare, the clearer my thinking is," she noticed. "I can feel my eyes open into the Clarity."

She made it a habit to go directly to her office after sitting in order to record any gifts from her moments by the pond before losing them to the return of her ordinary mind.

"The germ doesn't live very long," Mel thought as she trotted lightly through the morning mist. "I'd better not dally."

She slowed anyway.

Catching sight of Jason, she beamed, "Who would have thought he could make me feel this way?"

Mel enjoyed their walks. Her loneliness was gone, but there was more. Jason helped her think. He was a good listener, and Mel had found her thoughts became more coherent by talking them through.

"It won't get lost if we talk about it," she thought as he trotted up.

Jason began talking as they settled into their stroll. "I've been thinking. Look at how things have changed. First we moved from trying to strengthen our ability to control our

27

creativity. Now we're simply trying to open ourselves to participating in origin. But how?"

Mel paused, "Just by relaxing, I guess."

"What do you mean?"

"We have to relax the mental efforts that inhibit participating in origin."

"You mean we have to quit thinking?"

Mel grinned. "I hope not. But we have to quit thinking the wrong way. We know we can't control the mind with our understanding. We at least have to quit trying what we know doesn't work."

Mel felt a chill as Jason's voice became tense, "But what's the alternative? You do it so much. How do you get in?"

Mel felt her pulse begin throbbing. "He's pushing me," she thought. "I can't tell him about the pond. That's the only place I have to be alone. It's right under his nose, and he doesn't see it. This isn't right."

Turning to Jason, Mel said simply, "I really don't know."

"That's true enough," she thought to herself as she watched them stroll awkwardly along.

It was hard for Mel to tell if the ache in her stomach was coming from her or from Jason. "Probably both," she thought.

Mel's inspiration died, and the walk didn't last long. She wasn't surprised.

"I hope I don't lose him," she thought he disappeared into the morning mist.

**

Mel slid quietly from the building. "It won't be long now," she thought.

Mel was lucky for her secret door. She had noticed it one afternoon while sitting by the pond. Hidden by a tree fern, it was easy to miss. Ignoring the alarm sign, she had tried the door, which opened silently behind some shrubs on the rear wall of the atrium. Better still, it was unlocked.

"Perfect," she had said to herself. "I can check through the glass to see if anyone is on the other side. Now I have a private way to get to and from my spot. And I can come as early as I want."

By now she was familiar with every twig along the path, so she was comfortable as she passed through the darkness. Walking briskly away from the building, Mel found her cut through the woods to the trail. So long as she reached the trail before light, no one would be able to tell where she had entered.

Passing through the woods, her mind raced. "I feel like a kid running away from home. I wonder if he'll be there."

Stealing up to the trail, Mel saw a shape. It was Jason. As Mel watched him pace, her throat began to ache with tension that seemed to be coming from her chest. Ignoring this, she slid onto the trail behind the taut form.

"His breathing is heavy," she thought as she approached, "but he's not puffing. He's been here a while and he's worked up about something, probably us. At least he won't hear me coming."

Jason turned as she reached him. "I didn't hear you," he said tentatively. "I thought you might not be coming. I'm sorry about yesterday. I really didn't mean to be so invasive."

Mel's shoulders relaxed. "He's really been worried," she said to herself.

Turning to Jason, she spoke gently, "Don't worry. I know I'm a little too private sometimes, but I really enjoy being with you. My life is better for our conversation... and your company."

Jason's breathing relaxed. Smiling, they started to walk. Mel didn't notice when their hands came together.

By dawn they had nearly finished their first lap of the trails, and the talk had turned to research.

"So you're saying this disease doesn't originate in the mind," Jason was saying. "It comes from somewhere else. But where?"

Mel paused. "When we're filled with turmoil, thinking simply doesn't help. This says to me that it's coming from somewhere other than the mind. The point is, intellectual cures just don't work. Why do we keep wasting time trying to find something that we know isn't there? Even if we don't know the answer, we have to quit trying what won't work if we want to open ourselves to what will."

Mel froze in her tracks.

Jason released her hand gently.

Mel's face relaxed as she continued, "What will? That's the answer. The disease is getting to us through the will. We know we're not helped by our knowledge; as much as we know we still end up attacking ourselves. No matter how focused or how intelligent we are, we're still helpless. What does that mean? Our will is overpowering our mind. Whatever this disease really is, it doesn't come from the mind. It comes from the will. Cancer of the mind really is cancer of the will."

As she launched herself toward her office, Mel flashed a smile at Jason, "Thanks for everything. I've got to get this into the computer. See you tomorrow?"

"I hope so," he replied as she disappeared.

Mel's body tingled with excitement as she flew across the room to her computer. Flinging herself at the keyboard, the machine was alive in seconds.

The screen lit, ONE NEW MESSAGE.

"That's odd," she blinked. "Who would have been at work so early?"

"I sure don't want to read it now," she thought, bringing the message to the screen.

Staring feverishly, she tried to understand what she was seeing.

We recognize we were confused about where to look for control of the disease. We know we can't find it by bearing down intellectually. No amount of effort helps us when we need it most. The same thing happens when we have trouble in any creative activity. The harder we try the more we fail. But what does this mean? To me it says the control of cancer of the mind will come only when we surrender our efforts, not when we succeed in overpowering our mind. *Harley*

Poised at her keyboard, Mel felt her hands throbbing with her pulse. "There's no reason for me to be sweating," she thought. "I didn't run that far."

Fingers trembling, she started to type.

I agree. We have to look at the will. Whatever this disease is, it comes from the will, not from the intellect. Control of the disease has to come from control of the will. *Mel*

Almost immediately, her screen lit in return.

*Did you read my last message? I believe we can move toward a cure by surrendering our efforts. We know intellect isn't up to the job, and creativity is the only other mental function we know. But we don't <u>control</u> creativity; we just launch it. *Harley**

Mel's eyes had cleared by the time she typed her response.

*Call it what you want, but we aim it somehow. When Mozart sat to write a string quartet he didn't end up with a symphony. *Mel**

She knew his reply wouldn't take long.

*I know we need our intellect to set up tasks. So? Control still isn't related to actually participating in origin. *Harley**

Mel thought about this a while before beginning.

*Right. But it seems to me that the important similarity between our creativity and our resistance to the disease lies in how we set up our automatic responses. I believe the same things can get in the way of both activities. It feels the same to me. If I could pause before I fell into forcing things maybe it would help. This works when I'm writing. Maybe I could initiate a positive response to my mental compulsions the same way I initiate a creative responsiveness in my writing. In the end you can call it what you want. But if we're going to change our responses to difficulties we're going to have to control our impulse to do things the old way. *Mel**

"It'll take him a while to dig out of this one," Mel thought gleefully.

Her eyes widened as her screen lit immediately.

Inhibiting a negative response is a fine thing, but don't I remember you saying some time ago that we should be committed to finding a "positive" cure? Remember: "Positive =

*effective in establishing the right thoughts. Negative = effective in stopping the wrong ones." *Harley**

Mel's fingers were trembling again. Before she could respond, her screen lit again.

*So you're saying there's an active way to get past a creative block. And you think if we can actively move to participating in origin we can find relief from attacks of the disease. Fine. But how can we do this? *Jason**

Harley lunged back.

*I didn't say I knew how to do it. I thought we were past this debate. Didn't we agree a long time ago that it's stupid to keep trying methods we know won't work? *Harley**

Mel's heart pounded as she watched the screen. No reply.

Mel felt her shoulders drop. "He was just trying to protect me, and Harley knows it."

Finally her screen lit again.

*The point is that we do know some things about the disease. For instance, we know there are similarities between difficulties participating in origin and difficulties coping with attacks of cancer of the mind. So why not look for similarities in coping mechanisms? We know we simply cannot muscle our way into true origin. The harder we try, the more we fail. Isn't this exactly what happens when we try to turn our mind away from malignant thoughts? Successful artists must have a way of coping with this kind of difficulty, and I'll bet it doesn't come from trying to destroy the problem. I'll bet it comes from knowing how to just let go of it by replacing it with something else instead. How? I have no idea, but I don't believe it can be found in a muscular response. That's simply contrary to everything we've discovered. *Harley**

*Does this mean we're looking for an active way to open a passive responsiveness? *Jason**

*Maybe that's it. Maybe our mental muscle simply has to be trained to look for a trigger, not a handle. *Harley**

*What's the difference between a trigger and a handle? Aren't they both used actively and directly? *Jason**

Mel felt her hands begin to tremble again. Harley's reply brought relief.

*Yes. But look at how they work. We use handles to understand, predict, and control things. Triggers just launch things. We aim them, but once they are triggered they fly on their own. *Harley**

"I guess the sandbox fight is over," Mel sighed. Smiling, she began to type.

*So the object is to learn how to actually launch at what we want instead of what we're trying to avoid. *Mel**

*Precisely. Any suggestions? *Harley**

There was no reply.

Chapter 4

The Coot and the Glimpse

"It's hard to imagine how so much could have happened in so little time," Harley smiled wryly. "I don't suppose I can do more for my cause than he's already doing for me."

He looked at Jason's campaign. Only two weeks had passed since receiving the notice, but time was running out. Within a week they would have to elect a Research Administrator. Jason campaigned heavily for support, but the more he tried to win the favor of his colleagues the more feverish his efforts became.

"Just like always," Harley mused.

Harley reacted publicly by becoming more serene and detached than ever, but inwardly he watched anxiously as events unfolded. He breathed more easily when, in a last minute effort to salvage what was left of his dignity, Jason withdrew his candidacy a few days before the election.

Election day arrived with Harley as the only announced candidate, so it was a rude shock to him when Mel was elected. It shocked Mel too. She had voted for Harley.

Although everyone gave Harley a wide berth for a few days, his enthusiasm seemed undiminished. Within hours of the election he posted a message onto the network.

Why is it so natural to see our will as a product of mind? Mel's picture seems much more accurate. After all, if we claim that will is a product of rational intellect, we're saying that it can't exist independently of a rational mind. One look at nature tells us this is foolish. Many creatures devoid of rational capacity have strong wills.

*We can avoid the chicken and egg problem by simply continuing to look for a way to trigger the will. Now that we know the trigger has to connect with a capacity deeper and beyond the control of our understanding, we're at least pointed in the right way. *Harley**

There was a pause. No one wanted to take the chance of interrupting him before he was finished, especially now.

*It's amazing what we discover when we look carefully at the murky areas of our understanding! But the problem remains. What do we really know? We talk about the will as the root of the disease, but we still have no idea what we're talking about. Without a clear idea of what the will really is, we're liable to take another wrong turn. Any ideas? *Harley**

*Is it possible that the will is just our biggest bundle of desires? *Mel**

*There does seem to be a connection between desires and will, but what you're saying doesn't fit with experience. If there is no difference between desire and will, why would I ever be stuck thinking negative thoughts when I want more than anything else to be free of them? *Harley**

*Maybe we should distinguish between wanting and wanting to want. *Mel**

*Why? I don't see what this gets us. *Harley**

*This might explain the conflict between what we want and what we do. Sometimes we might not really want what we think we want. *Mel**

*So you're saying that even though I don't see it, I really want to be tormented. I don't think so. *Harley**

Mel was silent, but the debate went on. At first most people sided with Harley. Mel's idea gradually began to catch on but Harley remained unconvinced, and his aggressiveness increased as his support diminished.

"This is foolishness," he would say. "Desire is desire, period. You can't tell me that I don't really want what I feel I want. After all, wanting is only a feeling. It's just there. It's neither true nor false. It just is what it is, and it's only what it is because I feel it. How can it be anything other than simply what it seems to me when I feel it? If I want something I want it. If I don't, I don't. How can there be a difference between 'wanting' and 'wanting to want'? Both are examples of 'wanting', and whichever I am feeling is simply what I am wanting right now."

No one knew for sure, but some suspected it emerged because of Jason's feelings for Mel. Someone had to be the first to use it, and Jason certainly was clever enough to have coined the name. This didn't really matter though, since soon everyone seemed to be calling Harley "the Coot". It didn't take long for people to learn not to take the Coot on, especially after his public humiliation of Jason. The Coot was a formidable opponent, and it was evident that he had harbored a deep resentment for Mel ever since her promotion. He simply couldn't understand it in light of his seniority and superior qualifications.

When it finally became clear that the problem was not going to go away, Mel was forced to deal with the Coot directly. Reluctantly, she scheduled a meeting in a small lab in a building near his office.

Mel spoke first. "Why is it," she asked, "that you claim victory when you attack what we don't bother to defend? You claim there's no difference between 'wanting' and 'wanting to want', since both are examples of desire. We agree that this statement can say something that is true. But you assert from it that there is no need for our distinction, when experience clearly demonstrates not only that this distinction is real, but that it's useful as well."

Not wishing to be put on the defensive, the Coot interrupted. "How can you say that experience clearly demonstrates that this distinction is real, when my experience doesn't assert any such thing? Your assertions demonstrate the depth of your threat to this project. You pretend to argue when you merely assert your personal beliefs. And your beliefs are dangerous. You'd have us abandon rationality completely if we would let you. You lead a team of scientists and philosophers when you have no knowledge of scientific method, or of what constitutes evidence. How can we hope to succeed when you continually push us to chase the phantoms of your personal conjectures? We need to move toward a cure, yet we waste our time investigating whether there's a difference between 'wanting' and 'wanting to want'."

Mel's pulse pounded as she fought to conceal her fear. She barely controlled her voice as she began, "Very well. Let's suppose for the moment that you're right. My beliefs are invalid because they're not supported by the experiments of others. Since my beliefs are not corroborated by your own experience, for instance, my conclusions are incorrect. But isn't there another possibility? If we're attempting to follow scientific method, shouldn't we look carefully at whichever experiment disagrees most with the majority? If so, we must investigate yours.

You claim that you see no use for the distinction between 'wanting' and 'wanting to want'. I believe you. But have you looked clearly and completely, *and with an open mind*? Are you certain that you haven't overlooked something in your own experience that would demonstrate the correctness and usefulness of this distinction?"

Coot's face was red and he was trembling with rage. Mel knew she wouldn't get another chance, so she talked faster. "Not so long ago you thought you wanted nothing more than the success of the project. Yet you found when you were overlooked for my position that you really desired something even more than the success of the project. You wanted prestige, or power, or whatever else my position might have provided. Now you find yourself working actively against the progress of the research. You might say that the situation has changed, so your desires simply have changed as well, but that doesn't blunt my point. Look closely. The changing situation hasn't changed your desires, it simply has uncovered them. And they weren't merely hidden from the rest of us. They were hidden from you as well."

Coot's face went slack. After a moment, the old kindness of Harley's face returned. Mel relaxed as she continued. "Wouldn't you have been better off recognizing your hidden desire in the beginning, before your reaction of pride magnified it? Wouldn't you have had a better chance to resist if you had identified and resisted it before your desire erupted with such force? And doesn't this show ample reason for distinguishing between a desire that we want to have, and a desire that we truly have? Can't we fight our individual compulsions best by working to identify all of our little desires, accepting and transforming them before they gain enough strength to overpower us? But how can we do this if we deny that they exist? Yet this is exactly what we do when we deny the distinction between what we truly want and what we want to want. We can't change our desires unless we have something to work with, something to use to gradually begin the transformation. We *can* begin by changing what we want to want. Of course this doesn't finish things, but it's a way we can begin to move."

Mel stopped, and both were silent for a time. Finally Harley asked, "But what about the will? What is it really, and how can we make it our friend instead of our enemy?"

She answered, "I don't think the will is a thing we have to subdue or win over. In a sense, the will doesn't even exist. What we call cancer of the mind really is a product of our unwanted habits. Whether we see them or not, our habitual reactions are the source of our misery.

The will may be nothing more than the unfolding of focused and unopposed desire. Mental and physical actions may be just events in which desires are actualized through a moment in which they meet no opposition. So long as desires are in conflict, action is impossible. But the instant my desires are focused and unopposed, they are actualized. My focused and even momentarily unopposed desires are my will."

Harley saw that he was beginning to fall behind, so he groped for some way to slow Mel down without unsettling her. Finally he said, "But what about when I stumble? If all action merely is an unfolding of unopposed desire, why isn't it always smooth and competent?"

Mel said, "Competence depends on sustained focus. But conflicting desires may resurface, especially if they have yielded unwillingly. Whatever action springs into being is spontaneous, through an instant of focused accord, but this doesn't mean that all action is smooth and competent. Complex actions depend on a complex accord, and even the most familiar activities can become wooden and inept just through an involved activity of watching. It's not easy to walk across a stage.

You know, I remember when you said that the will couldn't be a product of mind. This makes a lot of sense, but I don't think I understood it completely before. I was assuming that my will *invariably* dominated my mind. Although this is true when I yield to my compulsions, I don't think it has to be this way. I really believe that the mind I'm seeing now can control my will. I think I know where to find a cure for the disease we're studying. We're not researching cancer of the mind or cancer of the will. We're researching cancer of the heart. Relief can come only through purification of heart.

For me this means purification of ego. It's clear to me now that freedom from compulsion comes only when I am free from my pride. Not because I'm suddenly above my pride. That's not really freedom. When my heart opens I'm free in a different way. I just don't need my pride for the moment. That's the way I'd like to be. Free of the need for my pride, and free of the needs and compulsions that go with it."

The two sat quietly for a while. Finally Harley asked, "I think I see what you mean. It's a lot easier to accept my failures when I look at things this way. After all, even when my heart was in the wrong place it was in the right place, in a sense. I really wanted to be working in the best interests of the project."

He paused before he went on, "I'm still not completely comfortable. My situation may have been easy. I really did *want* the project to succeed even in the heat of my self-involvement, but what about cases where compulsions seem attractive *after* their exposure? What if I had chosen to pursue my personal ambitions even after recognizing them? Could negative feelings with this kind of power really be healed?"

Mel breathed deeply, relaxing as she replied, "That's a tough one, but I think the principles would have to be the same. The tricky part would be to find some aspect of healing that you really wanted, even if you hadn't recognized your need. It's sad, but this isn't always possible in therapy. Bitterness can run very deep, and no one can heal unless they want to. And I think you're right when you put it the way you just did. It really isn't a question of curing. Mental turmoil has to be healed, and healing seems to be the same as any other participating in origin.

We set a stage and then have to surrender to the process. Curing is different. It can be forced, but it is mechanical and incomplete.

I think the principles apply to physical healing too. We set a stage by mobilizing our resources through rest and nutrition, and maybe we go after a level playing field by appealing to antibiotics or less conventional remedies. Then we just get out of the way by relaxing, and our body heals as we sleep."

"I understand, but how could you have approached me if I had wanted my compulsion?"

"I would have had to want absolutely nothing for myself. Even if my self-involvement were hidden from me, you would have spotted it because you weren't looking at me intellectually. So I would have had to become quiet enough to feel compassion for you before I approached you at all."

"Is that what you did just now?"

"I tried, but I didn't do very well. Whatever happened just now must have come from you. I don't know what I would have done if you hadn't really wanted to let down."

Harley looked her in the eye, "There has to be a way to address this directly. And if there is, it should be the center of our research. I think we're finally looking at the key to the whole thing."

Just then the door opened. Although the room had yielded to the twilight gathering outside, the person who entered made no attempt to turn on a light. As he passed a window, Mel recognized the lanky profile of Yew, the evening custodian. "What could he be doing here?" she thought. "He's so gentle, I've never known him to move with such purpose. Still, he has always seemed to be as honest as any person in memory. Perhaps I should just wait to see what he does when he discovers we're here."

Harley, sitting silently, seemed to be thinking the same thing. Neither was prepared for what followed. As it turned out, Yew was very aware of their presence. Moving quietly between them, he sat gently on the floor. As he lowered himself, he said quietly, "I see it's time for us to meet. I'm happy I was here for your meeting. This is an auspicious occasion for you as well as for the project. It's time to really begin."

She'd heard that voice before. Of course... the lifeboat... Tears welled in her eyes as she saw Yew for the first time.

Chapter 5

The Closet

Harley and Mel had much to discuss for a long while. The office where they had come together was closed temporarily for soundproofing and redecorating, although no one actually saw any work going on. Occasionally Harley or Mel could be seen going in or coming out, sometimes accompanied by the evening custodian. Otherwise, no activity at all seemed to center around the place. Gradually this became less of a lunch hour topic and people turned their attention elsewhere. After all, many more significant things were happening. Harley had moved to an office next door to Mel's. They even shared a private inner door. How this could happen was anyone's guess, but Harley did seem to have changed dramatically. Now he was disarmingly gentle, actually compassionate. He still seemed to have his former fire but he didn't display it so often, and it seemed different somehow when he did. Everything considered, it was no surprise to anyone when he was promoted to become Senior Administrative Advisor for Personnel.

Mel had changed too. She was quieter, and she seemed *very* happy. Not always, but even this seemed to be changing. Absolutely nothing seemed to get her down. A current of anticipation built gradually among the personnel. With all the speculation, everybody agreed on just one thing - something big was about to happen.

What missed common attention was the frequency of the trio's visits to the small locked laboratory they had come to call the "closet". In fact, Harley and Mel had a carefully arranged schedule so each was permitted several hours of uninterrupted time each day either to be alone or with Yew in the room. The fact that Yew was the only custodian made it easy to come and go in private. Over time they soundproofed and redecorated the room. The walls were painted light blue, and what little furniture had been in the room was removed, replaced by a thick gold carpet with a few large cushions. Since the closet was on the third floor, the outside window didn't need to be covered for privacy. Light pink drapes were opened during the day to allow the morning sun to shine directly on the West wall. In all, it was a particularly pleasing room. The air seemed alive with a peculiar quiet that would touch each of them as they entered.

This was no coincidence. Each of them nurtured the atmosphere regularly. Yew had been very clear about this from the beginning. "If you are constantly respectful of the atmosphere in this room," he had said, "it will become a sanctuary that can restore you when you have need. Even if you discount the energy of a sanctuary, there is a psychological switch that is tripped when we enter a space that is associated with habits of quiet. And there really is more. The energy is real, and it builds over time in any space that is regularly treated with reverence."

Yew had been helpful, but he was a strange man. He was very quiet, especially about himself. Although he didn't seem to be hiding anything, no information about his background ever seemed to come to light. Oddly, neither Mel nor Harley felt any real curiosity about this. It just didn't seem to be relevant, so it never surfaced as an issue. They talked about it a few times, but neither of them bothered to check Yew's Personnel file. Mel said it first, "Why bother, when what is important to us would never be in there anyway. What we need to know, he'll tell us."

Their trust seemed to have been there from the beginning. He was absolutely unflappable. On their first meeting in the closet, he smiled and drew a long breath before he began in his quiet Southern way. "Your coming together has opened each of

45

you to a taste of freedom. Look at how it happened. Each of you was opened to your experience by your ability to accept a gift. It's important to see such gifts clearly, so we should take a look at what happened just now."

He looked at Mel. "You arrived today with two burdens, and neither was related to why you set up this meeting. Your openness has provided the project with its most significant advances, but recently you've felt some new pressures that were really tying you up. Your administrative responsibilities have grown, occupying much more of your time than expected. Added to this, your colleagues have come to expect regular flashes of inspiration. They assume you will provide them with some new germ to develop whenever they have finished their current tasks. As research continues, their tasks are finished more and more quickly. It's no wonder that you've been drawn into trying harder and harder to connect with your inspiration, and it's no wonder that your efforts have failed.

You knew this, even though you didn't see it in the heat of your exertions. Harley's antagonism brought it to a head with a confrontation you couldn't ignore. You arrived today with deep resolve and less focus than you realized. Although you were not surprised when Harley's first response to your words had nothing to do with the issues you had come to discuss, you didn't expect it to be such a vicious *personal* attack. This startled you, causing you for the briefest moment to forget all your agendas and difficulties. You were brought for a moment to participate only in the present, and a moment was enough. Your desire to become open had become very deep. Even the slightest break in your wall of concentration was enough to permit such deeply felt desire to become actualized. Harley's abuse shook you enough to make you quit trying to focus for a moment. This was all you needed, since your exertions were the only obstacle that had to be overcome. His abuse broke your stride and opened you right up."

Stunned, Mel blurted, "Are you saying that abuse can be *good?*"

Yew replied, "Looking closely, we can see that everything has both a good and a bad aspect to it. Goodness and badness are, to a large degree, what we make of things. We can even see this in our mental miseries. They can be quite negative, but they also can be a blessing if they make us resolve to move away from our inner turmoil. Eventually we can want this freedom enough to find it.

Instead of looking at things as intrinsically good or bad, it might be more helpful to look in terms of their power to open us to freedom. When we do this our approach to everything in our lives changes, and events affect us in a more helpful way. In this sense, good and bad only refer to aspects of momentum. If something pushes us toward freedom from self-destructive compulsions it is good, and anything that pushes us away from freedom is bad.

It's really a spiritual thing. We can deny this, saying that freedom is simply a psychological state where we're free from harmful thoughts and desires, but how are we supposed to get to such a state? We all know how powerful the negative side of human nature is. If freedom from negative compulsions is possible at all, there's no way it will emerge from our human nature. The source of that kind of freedom must be greater than we are. You were right when you said compassion is the key. It creates a unique space. Anyone within that space, either as vehicle or passenger, is touched by quiet. And anyone who has the chance to look at this quiet from within can see that it is spiritual."

Yew turned to Harley. "You had a burden too, when you came today. Your honesty was buried beneath hidden desires. But as you sat with Mel, you experienced a liberating feeling. Her experience exposed you to compassion, and this enabled you to accept a glimpse of freedom. You should know that even though Mel was instrumental this gift didn't come from her, and it didn't come from me. But this doesn't matter. What *does* matter is that you accepted it.

Your experience, just as Mel's, came when you least expected it. It didn't come because you were looking for it, and it didn't come because you worked hard enough at it to succeed. Try to remember this in your practice. Striving just doesn't work. The secret is in yielding. This happened at the moment when you were touched by compassion.

Always be on the lookout for compassion. With practice, you will be able to find it even when you're angry. This is a real blessing, and the greatest miracle you will ever experience. Other experiences may seem more spectacular, but no miracle is greater than the simple turning of a single hard feeling toward compassion. This is a good way to center your practice.

The two of you will have a lot to discuss as time passes. It's important for each of you to have someone who allows you to talk openly about things of substance, and this room will help you. You may wish to call it your laboratory, but it would better to draw as little attention as possible to this place. Then you can come here for quiet. Until your purification is complete, this will work well as a closet workshop."

He turned back to Mel. "In time you won't find your responsibilities so distracting, but when this happens, you will find yourself with new and even heavier responsibilities instead. You should consider relinquishing as many of your tasks as you can. Harley can help you with this. There are many things he can do as well as you. He certainly should have direct responsibility for personnel. Few people would approach him as discourteously as some have done to you. Your talents are for discovery, not personnel administration. As much as you can, you should put them to this use."

Finally he said to Harley, "Remember, you can still be a dragon without actually hurting anyone. No one needs to know that you're harmless. Your value to Mel is your ability to shelter her from the distraction of personnel issues, and your fire is essential for this. But even this isn't your real purpose. Your biggest value to the project is your ability to realize purification and healing within yourself. Do your tasks, but do them as practice. Practice approaching others without looking for something for yourself. You will be working with a lot of folks who have problems they can't see. This will be your chance to practice compassion. Look beyond what they think they want and feel their real yearning. Learn to see the real issues behind their inner and outer confrontations. Learn to feel what they feel as clearly as they feel it themselves, but know *why* they feel it. And never slip into sympathy. Learn to weep instead, and respond with compassion. Weeping is a wonderful experience. It lets us slip away from the psychological hardness and compulsions that isolate us from our compassionate nature.

We can weep with or without tears. It doesn't matter because the real weeping goes on inside, effortlessly. Weeping is an easy way to find peace and joy. Practice this, and you'll find yourself healing as you bring healing to others."

Mel interrupted, "How can you say our nature is compassionate? Mine certainly isn't, and I don't see how anyone else's nature is any different."

"Your nature is human like anyone else's. But I wasn't talking about your human psychological nature. I was referring to your real nature. Live with your practice a while and you will agree."

Yew slowly began to stand, "My job as evening custodian will guarantee the privacy of this area for much of each day. We can meet any evening you wish. I'll be here."

All of a sudden Mel had to ask, "Do you know Marjorie?"

He smiled, "Yes. She's been a friend to you more than once."

Mel pressed on. This was not what she had expected, but she did not want to be deflected.

"How is she?"

"Marjorie is very fine."

"Can you tell me anything about her? How do you know her?"

"I've been her friend for many years. All that matters is that she is genuine. We're fortunate to be her friends."

Mel asked, "Do you know what she did for me?"

"Yes."

"Why did she do it?"

"It was perfectly natural. You deserved and needed it."

"I appreciate that more than I can say, but can you tell me anything at all about Marjorie? I know nothing about her, and I owe her so much. Will I ever see her again?"

Yew smiled. "I'm sure you will. But much waits to be done in the meantime."

Before she could ask more, he turned and slipped quietly from the room.

Mel and Harley sat for a long while. Finally they stood and left without a word, locking the door behind them. The closet immediately became the silent center of research.

Chapter 6

Unquestioned Answers

Mel arrived in her office early the next morning. By the time the clerical staff arrived, she had located suitable office space for them on the floor below and had arranged for their equipment to be transferred so the actual move could be made over the following weekend. She also had been assured that their old office adjoining hers would be ready for Harley at the same time. This required a lot of work, but Mel had many supporters who were happy to help her with anything she needed.

And as it turned out, Harley had supporters as well. A few had been surprised when he was overlooked for the position of Project Administrator. This made the transition of power very smooth and enabled the project to move on without pause.

Meanwhile, Mel and Harley were busy. Their new work schedules seemed to agree with them. In addition to a full day working with the rest of the staff, they took independent shifts morning and evening in the closet. This puzzled them at first. Harley asked Mel, "Why does Yew want us to practice separately, when he told us we should be helping each other?"

"You're asking the wrong person. It doesn't make any sense to me either. Why don't you ask him when you see him this evening?"

Yew usually was easy to find when they arrived at the closet. Although he didn't seem preoccupied with them, he always seemed to be nearby whenever they had a question. They looked forward to this, because he turned out to have an unusually sunny disposition. After the heaviness of their first meeting, this was a pleasant surprise. They enjoyed watching their feelings of urgency yield to his quiet humor.

He didn't seem to look for conversation. He was happy and enthusiastic when he talked, but he didn't seem to have any particular need to say anything. Most of the time he was quite content with his custodial responsibilities. This seemed puzzling at first.

Harley was in a particularly good frame of mind when he arrived with his question. As expected, Yew was sweeping the hall near the closet. The lanky figure smiled as Harley approached.

After the usual greetings, he asked, "Mel and I were wondering why you want us to use the closet separately. Couldn't we help each other more if we practiced together?"

"Not really. The biggest help you can give each other as beginners is to kindle each other's enthusiasm, and this can be done very well outside the closet. Each one of us comes to our practice with individual obstacles to overcome. You've discovered that healing depends on becoming transformed. In time all of your habits will change. But for the moment if you look honestly you'll see that you believe you can do something special, something active, to help Mel succeed while she is practicing. Until you realize this isn't true you can help her best by supporting her with your enthusiasm and quiet compassion. This doesn't have to be done in the closet. You can do this very well over tea. In the end, you both will be helped more, and you certainly will get to enjoy more tea." Yew smiled and turned to a dust pile that beckoned. Harley went into the closet as Yew bent back to his work.

Within minutes, Mel arrived. Yew spoke first, "Harley already asked your question, but we can still talk. Why don't we walk outside? That way we won't distract him in the closet."

Yew stared into the distance as they passed into the cool outside air. Seeming to talk to no one in particular, he asked, "Do you believe in God?"

Mel was taken by surprise. After a pause, she answered quietly, "Yes."

"Fine. But what does this mean? What do you refer to when you use that word?"

Mel drew a deep breath as she replied, "I used to think it meant a person. But now I guess I just think of a Force."

"What attributes would you associate with this Force?"

Mel's reply came slowly, "I guess love."

"Good. Does anything else come to mind?"

After a long pause, Yew continued, "How about Mind?"

Mel was silent, so Yew continued, "Looking at what happens between us, how we share experience without words or actions, it's not much of a stretch to picture a Universal Mind deeper than the intellect we cultivate as individuals. But we can't see this with our intellect. Intellect looks at the surface of things. That's what it's for. Real Mind is simply deeper than intellect can see."

"You mean so deeply buried my intellect isn't powerful enough to see it?" Mel asked.

"Not exactly," Yew continued. "This kind of depth is different. It's not a thing we can look at. We simply have to experience it to know it."

Mel's head was swimming. "Does he really expect me to understand this?" she thought.

"I'm sorry it doesn't make more sense now, but it will," Yew responded calmly.

Mel's pulse pounded as her mind raced, "Can he read my thoughts?"

He replied immediately, "It's not like that. I just experience what you are experiencing through empathy with the forming ground of your thoughts. Sometimes words come to mind, but they seem more to be shared outgrowths from a common source than something taken from your mind."

"How do you do it?"

"I don't." Seeing her confused look he added, "Really."

"Then explain." Mel was startled by the raspy edge of her voice.

Yew smiled and settled into his soft drawl, "It just happens naturally. Remember the Depth we were just talking about? You don't have to believe this, but for a moment imagine that what we usually think is mind really is just an outgrowth of a larger Mind. My personal mind is an individual object, part of a universe of objects in this Cosmic Mind. We can call this Cosmic Mind "God" if we wish. Now we're looking at God the way you do, as a Force. Universal Mind is simply a way of describing that Force."

Yew turned toward an imposing old tree as the trail wound back once again to their building. Set on the crest of a hill, the building was dwarfed by the majestic old oak. Mel saw a bench nestled beneath its huge branches. The limbs that formed the vaulted ceiling were nearly 20 feet above her head, bending gracefully to the ground on all but one side, which was open enough for a nice view of the sky. The bench faced out through the opening to an uncluttered view of the horizon to the East. "What a wonderful place to watch the sunrise," she thought through her smile.

Yew moved toward the bench as he continued, "Let's sit for a while. This is a peaceful spot, good for looking at things clearly."

As they settled onto the bench, he went on, "You know, the Mind we're talking about now is quite different from my personal mind tied to a physical brain. In this larger picture, Mind is the source of all being, the existence shared by all the brains and minds and other things we find in the universe."

"Aren't we back to the guy in the sky?" Mel asked with a dry grin.

She was shocked as Yew returned her look. Then he gave her a relaxed smile and continued, "Only if that's what we really want. But we don't have to picture somebody doling out shares of stuff called existence. We can *look another way* if we wish."

"I recognize my own words," Mel said. "What are you trying to tell me? How are we supposed to look?"

"Non-dualistically."

"What do you mean?"

"By looking at origin this way, seeking to experience it as a wellspring, we take a step toward non-dualism. We're at least not looking at a personality with intellectual intentions. We're closer to seeing God as an infinite Force."

"Okay, I guess. But I still don't see how this helps me see God non-dualistically, or even why it is important."

"It moves us toward opening our heart eye. God looks different when we think in terms of a wellspring instead of a decision-maker. Hopefully the view is different enough to push us into letting go and really seeing.

As soon as we think we recognize something, we turn away from our intuition and start analyzing instead. We see what we've learned to expect. This blocks us from completely seeing what's there. But if we simply relax our mind instead, we become open to Depth. I'm just saying what you've already said to others. Looking another way doesn't mean looking in another direction, it means using, opening into, another way of looking. Then our eyes turn automatically in the right direction, and we see with Clarity."

"Okay, but even if I understood this, which I don't, how does this get me away from dualism?"

"No one ever really understands Depth in the conventional sense. It doesn't matter. We don't need to understand it. The point is, when we open to Clarity we're seeing non-dualistically. That's just the way it happens."

Mel felt her spirits sag as these words sank in. Looking at Yew, she knew he was speaking from experience. "But how does this help me?" she thought. "It's a closed circle. So what if Clarity and non-dualism go together? They're both beyond reach for me. It seems more hopeless than ever."

Then she noticed Yew's eyes. They were open, but they seemed fixed on the distance as he looked gently through her, and his face seemed to glow. As she noticed this, she felt herself relax, surrendering to warmth that was sweeping through her. She watched herself begin silently and effortlessly to weep, sensing an invisible veil forming over her head then painlessly moving down through her entire body. She felt her inner tensions dissolve with the passing of the veil.

Gradually she became aware of a thin blue light from Yew's right eye to her left. She closed her eyes, gradually opening just her right eye. The light was gone. Closing the right, she opened her left eye again to find the light still there. Repeating this several times, the result was the same.

By this time her mind had become active. "I wonder if this means the right eye is the transmitter and the left is the receiver. Does this mean the right eye is positive and the left eye is negative?"

"You know the answer without asking. Don't think about it."

Mel realized she had no idea if either of them had actually spoken a word. Relaxing again, she smiled quietly at Yew and settled into another moment of quiet.

"I'm beginning to realize how I can know something without understanding," she finally said.

"Good. You have enough experience. Think about what happens when we share thoughts. We don't need to understand. We just know."

Mel smiled tentatively. "I still can't imagine how my mind could be so blind to its own origin."

"Just pretend you're asleep and dreaming about yourself. In your dream your mind has quite a few ideas of its own. But all your dream ideas, your whole dream world, exist only because of your waking mind, even though your dream mind doesn't see this. Now look at yourself as you sit here, awake. It's not hard to imagine a real Mind that we can't see any more than our dream mind can see our waking mind.

We can learn to see our waking mind as we dream by bringing our waking awareness into dream. But our dream mind can never see our waking mind on its own. In the same way, real Mind can see our waking mind along with our dream world. But our intellect doesn't have the power to see the real Mind of its own origin on its own. We can come to accept reality, but not through our power of deduction. Intellect can analyze things to rule out conclusions that are wrong, but it doesn't have the power to discover what is beneath the surface of experience.

Looking at our dream mind again, it is blind to its origin. Unless it becomes empowered by the intervention of our waking mind through lucid dreaming, it simply can't see the truth beyond its dream world. And our waking mind is powerless in the same way. It must be empowered by its ground in order to see the truth of its origin as well. Otherwise, in a real sense, we're still only dreaming."

The friends sat quietly for a long while. Eventually Yew turned to Mel, speaking softly. "When we die, what dies?"

She waited for words to come. "Body. But what about mind? How could my mind and personality survive the death of my brain?"

"They don't. At least not in the way you're thinking right now. Your ordinary mind is linked with your brain and physical body. Your body and your intellectual mind die together."

"So soul doesn't exist, and my individual being dies with my body."

"I didn't say that. There is more than one way that thinking goes on. In a real way, this means that there is more than one kind of mind. You know that you can't do certain kinds of things with your intellectual mind, but you are discovering that your elusive creativity can do everything. Intellectual tasks as well as creative ones are within its power.

Creativity is a portal to the Mind that transcends death. It doesn't matter if our ordinary intellectual mind dies with our body. True Mind, the real Mind that underlies it all, does not depend on our physical body for its existence. It really is the other way around. Our existence, all existence, emanates from the power and love of this Mind.

We live in a universe of depth. There are several levels to this depth, but we usually stare just at the surface. This is the physical level, or physical plane of existence. It includes all the material stuff of the universe and more. The line folks like to draw between physical and mental stuff is confusing, because the physical level of existence actually includes all the intellectual stuff as well. This is just good common sense, because we can see that our intellectual mind is inseparable from our brain as we live our life in a physical world.

Thankfully, we don't have to limit ourselves to looking just at the surface of things. If we really want, we can let go of our old way of looking. When we become able to yield our intellect to the Mind that underlies it, the fabric of the universe becomes transparent and we see things as they really are. Then, no matter who we are, we discover the same thing. Fearlessness, unity, and bliss, all floating in unbounded love."

Mel relaxed and yielded to a tingling feeling beneath her skin. She watched as it swept silently from her feet to her head.

Then her old thoughts began to reassert themselves. Tensing, she looked at Yew, "I want to believe this, but how can I believe in a universe built on love when I see so much unfairness. Why do horrible things happen to good people? Where's the love in that?"

"There is a reasonable picture that resolves these problems. It may not be comfortable, because it comes from another culture. But it is rational, and it resolves the conflicts between what we'd like to believe and what we see around us. Have you ever heard the word 'karma'?"

"Yes, but I can't recall offhand exactly what it means."

"What goes around, comes around. The love that floats the universe is unflinchingly fair."

He paused, watching Mel. Staring at the ground, she finally broke the silence. "That's a wonderful thought, but I still don't see how it fits with reality."

"I know. But you *can* see if you really want. You're trying to balance on too small a patch of ground. This is perfectly natural. You've been taught to be afraid of accepting support that might come from beyond the perimeter of a very narrow circle of faith. And you've been taught that faith requires denial of common sense. This means you have to have two hats, a religious hat and a scientific one. But this calls for two faces as well. No one really finds this comfortable. If we're ever going to have real faith, it must stand the test of open examination. Intellectual belief alone isn't enough for faith, but it has to be a part of it. We can't really believe anything that is obviously self contradictory."

Mel broke in, "I've felt this for a long time. When I was a child I wasn't allowed to ask certain questions. I couldn't understand why no one would let me ask what I needed to ask, because without asking how could I really believe what I was told to believe? I finally realized that they really didn't care <u>if</u> I believed anything at all. They only cared <u>what</u> I believed if I chose to have beliefs. In the end they just wanted to keep me from making it hard for them to believe what they were afraid not to believe.

What you're saying is really helpful. But where does it go from here? How do I reconcile my idea of a loving universe with the injustice I see all around me?"

"We can't explain the hardships of any one lifetime just in terms of itself. But if we step back and look at a larger picture we can watch the scales of justice balance. I don't mean just to look at the whole universe instead of the individuals in it. This makes no sense, because everybody's worth is denied if there is no worth in each one of us. But there is a way. We need to look at justice in terms of a longer expanse of time. After all, the results of our actions aren't always immediate."

"Are you going to tell me heaven is the reward that justifies undeserved misery here? That just makes things worse, because it makes a mockery of human life. Why do some innocent people have to suffer while other good people are spared here and now?"

"Are you familiar with the meaning of reincarnation?"

Mel shuddered.

He continued, "It's hard to look at this without flinching, it goes so much against what we're told we should believe. But let's set our worries aside for a moment and take a careful look to see what makes sense. Our experience can either help us or hurt us here. Even though it can be unsettling when our experience pushes us away from what we've been taught, we have to let it open our eyes to what is really going on."

Mel said, "I can accept the idea of reincarnation when I remember what I've just learned about Mind, but it's still hard for me to really believe that my soul travels from one body to another."

Yew said, "Fine. Just keep looking. After all, we can't imagine even an ordinary mind without memory. So if my existence as an individual mind and personality emerge from infinite Mind, it's not hard to imagine being held in a memory that can recall my essence to physical being many times."

"So you're saying that even though our individuality doesn't endure on the physical plane, it is held in Mind, in which, through which, it exists."

"Yes. And so long as my individual being clings to any desire, it never ceases to exist in its individual essence. In other words, it continues to exist as an individual as long as I want it to. Eventually when we reach a certain point of light and peace our desires have nothing to hook onto, so we simply dissolve into the causal Mind. But we don't have to worry about this happening without our permission, because so long as fear remains, so do we."

Mel was uneasy, but she said nothing as Yew continued.

"We glimpse causality, some call it the ground luminosity, when we die. If we recognize and embrace it freely, we let go of the wheel of birth and death. But until we've glimpsed causality we can't recognize it. And even if we have experienced glimpses we may flinch away from it in fear, mainly fear of losing our individuality.

It takes more than a few glimpses of truth to get us to quit clinging to our personalities. A glimpse is a trickle of truth. It may inspire us with its Clarity, but the View is obscured rapidly by the dust and clutter of the world as soon as our habits come back into play. This changes though, little by little. Each glimpse changes our habits a little more, until eventually we realize we're free."

Mel sat without responding. Yew finally broke the silence. "You can ask anything you want. Don't be afraid of offending me with an honest question."

"Okay. I really think I understand how the idea of reincarnation responds to the problem of evil coming into the lives of people who don't seem to deserve it. Supposedly I'm free to see a God that is neither powerless nor nasty, but the problem really hasn't disappeared for me. Now I have to believe that everybody who has problems in life is a bad person who is being repaid for past sins. I just can't believe this about everybody who has to suffer. Many people who suffer seem to have very gentle spirits, and this just doesn't fit. On top of this, it seems extremely negative to say that I deserve every abuse that comes to me unbidden. The whole idea seems repulsive. As a psychologist I'm spending my life trying to help people find wholeness and happiness. Now I'm being told I'm supposed to tell them they should feel guilty when someone abuses them. I can't do this."

"That's an honest objection, and I'm happy to respond. The idea of reincarnation needn't discourage personal recovery at all. Regardless of what we believe about reincarnation, life is a game of balance much like walking from one end to the other of a tightrope. According to the doctrine of reincarnation, we lose our memory of the real truth beyond the game once we step onto the rope. While we carry skills from other games we have forgotten, we also enter each game with a burden. In one way or another our burden always is a burden of choice. Most choices were made inadvertently during other forgotten games. But we can enter a game also with extra burdens chosen intentionally in moments of clarity between games. Each of us has the option to carry a larger burden than necessary in any given game. The only real rule, the one of justice, compels us to carry what we deserve from our past. Because it is a just rule, we are given only so much as we can bear to carry in our sack at one time. There is freedom though, so old and skilled souls can choose to carry heavier or especially active burdens in addition to what is given by the rule.

This can be dangerous if they do not maintain their balance to the end of their given life-timeline. But so long as their heart looks to the real purpose of their life they will not fall far, and much can be gained by balancing such a burden successfully to the far end of the line. Even an awkward passage under such a load brings great purification and progress. The real danger comes to those who lose sight of life's purpose. They can fall far, causing them to begin the next game with a burden so light that progress is once again very slow.

The game itself plays out as we try to balance our burden from one end of our lifeline to the other. Our passage is complicated by our own distractions along with the activity of others. The activity around us can cause our line to shake unexpectedly. Sometimes others will even shake our line deliberately, but even though the space of our life is filled with disruption and activity we occasionally find someone who will reach out to steady our line. Even one whose energy is part of our sack of burdens can reach out with compassion to steady our line. They are, after all, growing too. And their line is likely to be particularly close to our own. Life is a strange game, but it can be very beautiful when we look clearly."

Mel raised her head, forcing herself to look into Yew's eyes. Her pulse was pounding, "This all makes sense, but why isn't it possible to look at this from a Christian point of view? Why do I have to build my faith through the traditions of another culture when I have Christ's example and offer of love and salvation in my own? And what about the idea that salvation depends on following Christ alone?"

Yew smiled, but instead of replying he stared silently into the distance. Mel started to talk, but there was something about Yew that pulled her up before she made a sound.

After a while, he looked at her and said, "Thanks. It's nice to be quiet for a while every now and then. A lot of folks are uncomfortable with silence. They think they're being considerate, taking me off the hook because maybe I can't think of what I want to say. They don't see that they're the ones who are uncomfortable. It's too bad when people are uncomfortable with silence, because things tend to improve when we quiet down every now and then."

I'll answer your question, but right now your eyes are glazed and you need to relax. Your brain has just been put through a lot, and you need to get a second wind. Just take a few breaths of fresh air."

Mel smiled and snuggled into the bench. Afternoon was just settling into dusk. As the world became quiet, so did she.

"Just take a long slow breath," she heard. "Let it feel cool and delicious. Then before the gate closes at the top, let it seep out on its own. Just let go of your eyes and your belly and relax. Let your tension float away through the air."

Mel felt a wash of relief flowing from her head downward. When it reached her chest it stuck on her old familiar knot. Pushing, she couldn't get it past the knot.

Yew's voice filtered in again, "Don't go after it. You're not after success. You're after relief. Just relax, and let it find you. Take another breath. Drink the cool air, and pause at the top. Pause and relax before you let the air begin to seep. Don't begin to exhale. Just relax and the air will begin to seep on its own. You won't even feel it. Then let yourself relax even more as you settle into the space at the bottom. Remember, relief isn't in the air at the top, it's in the space at the bottom."

Mel felt her chest relax as she surrendered to the quiet.

When she opened her eyes, the sky was filled with stars. Yew was speaking, "A lot of folks talk about meditating, and some of them say some pretty strange things. Remember how you just felt. That's what meditating really means. Now I'll tell you what I believe about Christ's words.

In the first place, I think we have to understand Christ's words in light of his life and teachings. He went against the legalism of his time by living and teaching inclusive, unconditional, love. So we can't assume he meant for his blessing to be exclusive and restricted by legalistic ritual and intellectual belief.

It might be easier to see what's going on if we take a look through another tradition. After all, Christians aren't alone in their exclusive claims. The Bhagavad Gita contains an account of Krishna. Krishna is the Hindu Incarnation of Love, and in the Gita he says that the way to God is through him alone.

I can't believe that Krishna is asking for worship of his corporeal body, or even for worship of his non-corporeal personality. As an Incarnation of God, he's asking for devotion to the Divine that is manifest through him.

We can understand Christ's words the same way. Even though it's inspiring to see God in the personality and form of the Incarnation, we can understand Christ's words best by looking in light of the centrality of Spirit in his life and teachings. He taught of a spiritual, not a physical, kingdom. If we believe this, we can see that the way to the Father is through the Holy Spirit made manifest to us through the Son, and Christ showed that this is a Holy Spirit of pure and unconditional love. Unconditional enough to be given even to those who slew his body. This is a deeper and less exclusive meaning than the one we sometimes are taught, and it rings true to his life and the spirit of his teachings."

Mel said, "This makes sense. After all, what good are his words if they don't soften our hearts and open us to grace? Why else would he have said them? Christ lived and taught compassion, and compassion comes when I lower barriers, not when I become defensive."

"That's absolutely true," Yew said. Traditions that equally produce love, compassion, and humility don't have to be mutually exclusive. On the human level it's easy to see old institutions clinging to life by insisting that any other path will lead to an eternity of torment. There isn't a single Protestant denomination free from attack from within the Protestant family itself. But I can't see a reason for all this conflict in Christ's words if we look at them in light of his life and teachings."

He looked at Mel. "Take another breath. This time keep your eyes open. Look at the tree in front of you. Now let yourself be drawn into the space it sits in."

Mel breathed deeply, pausing at the top and noticing how tense she had become. She let the air spill gently as she dropped her belly. Then she began again. This time the air was cool and sweet. Pausing at the top, she relaxed more. She felt her mind become clear as she relaxed. Startlingly clear.

Yew's voice drifted to her, "Don't think about it. Just let yourself be for a while."

After a while, Yew's voice began again, "In the end you don't have to build your faith through the traditions of another culture. But you don't have to be afraid of other traditions either. Faith grows whenever a heart opens to the Grace of compassion, and there is no difference between a Christian, or Buddhist, or Hindu experience of compassion. God really is Love, so when faith is complete we don't see a difference between the God of Krishna and the God of Christ."

Mel interrupted, "So you actually can see the same love, and the same God, in Krishna and in Christ?"

"I'm not saying that if I look hard enough I can see it that way. I'm saying it's impossible for me to see it any other way."

Mel took a breath, started to speak, then just settled back into the bench. Yew rose after a few moments, smiling to her as he slipped back into the building.

Chapter 7

Happiness and Happiness,
Pain and Pain

Harley looked at Mel, setting his cup down as he spoke, "You know, these moments are becoming really important to me. There are fewer and fewer people I can really talk to. I feel stifled somehow when I talk with most people, even old friends. And most of the time I don't feel good after talking, just drained and agitated."

Mel said, "Me too, and I think I've figured out why.

Yesterday I visited with one of my oldest friends. We had a wonderful time. We talked about the kinds of things we've talked about for years, but after she left I noticed I was extremely agitated. Thinking about it later, it seemed strange. Sally didn't have any unusual problems. In fact, she was extremely happy. So I started looking at myself instead. In the end I couldn't find anything unusual about my feelings. I was happy for my friend, just like always. And then I finally realized that this was the whole point. I was feeling like I used to when I thought I was happy, but being agitated with a knot in my gut doesn't seem happy to me any more. I almost prefer the feeling I get when a little setback quiets me down. There are moments when it seems to push me into a calm that is really wonderful."

She stopped and sat quietly for several minutes. Harley warmed with appreciation for her and for the closeness that had come to them in a few short weeks.

Finally she spoke. "Doesn't it seem strange to think that happiness could depend on avoiding enthusiasm? Why do I have to be miserable when I'm enthusiastic about something? Originally I was trying to ease the miseries of my dark moments. Now it seems like my light moments are infected too. I have no idea what is going on. All I can say is that things look really different, and I'm not sure I like what I'm seeing. I'm going to talk to Yew." She was out the door before she finished talking. Harley just let her go.

Although it was early in the afternoon, she found Yew sitting on their bench under the old oak tree, staring into the distance. Approaching quietly, she was sure he knew she was there. She sat gently on the bench, waiting patiently for several minutes. As she sat, she gradually relaxed. "Really," she thought, "there's nothing nicer than just sitting here like this for a while. It's so peaceful. I don't really have to be doing anything else right now or I wouldn't have come here."

As she sat thinking, she was surprised to find herself removing her watch and hiding it in her pocket where she wouldn't be tempted to check it. As peculiar as this was for her, she noticed that she did it without her usual inner chatter. She smiled. It felt good to be away from the noise. Not even her watching brought it back. Over and over, thoughts began as feelings and dissolved before they coalesced into words. At one point she found herself thinking, "I don't need to finish this." Then she found herself feeling this without thinking any words whatsoever.

Finally she felt something that was entirely new. A headache had been building all day. It was the kind that came whenever she felt really stressed, and she watched it wash away in the wonderful feeling.

A flash of something passed. Was it outside or inside? She felt a surge of open joy, free from the diffusion and grasping that usually marked her moments of happiness. She felt completely whole for the first time.

She knew that the concepts she usually used to understand things wouldn't help her here. Things were absolutely clear, but they got murky again whenever words intruded, so she just relaxed. She knew words couldn't capture what she was experiencing anyway, but this didn't matter because she was sure she could discover it again whenever she wanted. Watching like a child, she saw her old feelings floating on the surface, of what? Something deeper... In that instant Mel realized who she really was.

After a while Mel gradually opened her eyes to see if Yew was ready to talk. She was surprised to see him standing silently in front of her under a dark starry sky. He drawled softly, "Hi Mel, did you have something you wanted to ask?"

"Not just now," Mel said softly. "Thanks."

Yew turned toward the building and she felt herself relax again as she stared into the night sky. She sat a long while, passing in and out of Clarity as she familiarized herself with the feelings that allowed her in. Eventually she slowly stood. She continued to practice as she meandered home.

The night passed quickly. Yew had mentioned lucid dreaming in passing. Since then, she had been noticing an increasing awareness during sleep, gradually coming to control her dreams with her inner dialogue as she dozed. But tonight was different. She began to dream, then fell directly into deep sleep.

Eventually she awakened completely revitalized and deliciously relaxed. Then, to her surprise, she watched as she relaxed even more. As she sank back in, she knew she wouldn't go back to sleep. It was as though she reached an invisible fork in the path of relaxing that normally ended in sleep, a juncture she had passed countless times without realizing. But she knew this time would be different. She had come to this fork many times as she practiced on the bench, so she knew there was no point in trying to see the path as it turned inward. Instead, she allowed herself to touch the feelings she recalled so vividly from the night before. Opening herself to these feelings, she felt her awareness shift in what she later would call the "flip" as her mind came alive in Clarity. Her headache, which was just beginning to arrive with the rain outside, was washed away in the grace of the moment that continued as she moved into her day.

Strangely, her day was marked by failures. It seemed to Mel that she failed more times than she could count. It happened every time a duty or distraction would involve her in habitual responses. This pained her more and more as the day ground on. She noticed how stealthily the diffusion could enter her mind, but seeing this didn't help very much. Her little successes were especially distracting. At tea that afternoon she brought it up with Harley.

Although he was disappointed when he found that she hadn't asked Yew about yesterday's question, he recognized quickly that his best bet was just to let her go wherever she wanted to go. So he sat quietly and let her talk.

"When I was worried about losing my enthusiasm, I visualized a drab existence. Without life's ups and downs, it seemed pointless. Then I thought of Yew. He's incredibly quiet, but he's the most spontaneous and enthusiastic person I've ever known.

I realized I was asking the wrong question. I guess this was because I had never experienced enthusiasm without the excitement and self-involvement that usually go along with it. For my whole life I had looked at the surface when I thought I was seeing what was underneath. The excitement that comes from most success is enthusiastic, but it's agitated too. I don't think this means that the activity is bad, but what I want to feel now is just the enthusiasm, without the agitation.

After a pause, she continued. "I was watching myself this morning. I had meetings with five different people. I saw five different agendas, each one favoring the project as well as the individual with whom I was talking. By the time I reached the fifth meeting I'd watched myself fail four times. Not very badly, but I did fail. Then I recalled that each failure had come when I'd forgotten to pause and quiet down before responding. And each time, the other person had flinched and hardened in response. Despite my best efforts, I was leaving a wake that was affecting whoever was on the other side of my desk.

The last meeting was the hardest. I guess I scheduled it that way so the others wouldn't have the disadvantage of following someone who had set me off. In any case, I steeled myself as I waited for him to begin. Then I realized that I didn't need to do this. He wasn't the real issue. I was. I knew that I didn't exactly have a winning streak to worry about this morning, and I really just wanted to glide through the rest of my morning without leaving a wake. So I centered more easily than I had all morning and let myself really hear what he was saying.

I noticed how involved he was, but my chest didn't tighten when this happened. I just took in his involvement along with everything else. Then, when he had finished his argument I noticed myself smiling a real smile, probably the first genuine smile I had ever found when he was near. I found myself enthusiastically looking at his proposal from *his* viewpoint, but with the ability to see a few things he had missed because I was looking without his self-involvement, and without my own. His response took me completely by surprise. He relaxed and within minutes we came to an agreement that left us both smiling like old friends."

"Kind of like our meeting in the closet," Harley interjected.

"Yes," Mel went on, "but this time I was watching what was going on. It was gratifying to see the way pure enthusiasm works. It was as though I was just floating along. When an obstruction appeared the flow just carried it along. He couldn't be affected by my wake because we were both in the same flow. It was a wonderful moment, and I knew it wouldn't have happened if I had been pushing for anything at all for myself. And then I realized that *he* hadn't seen his self involvement any more than I had seen mine in our past encounters."

Harley flinched. "Are you sure? I think I know who you're talking about, and he seems to be pretty aware of his self-centeredness."

"It doesn't matter," Mel replied. "I know some people who approach me are aware of their selfishness, but I don't believe anyone who is selfish sees it all. I think Clarity is impossible when we're self-involved. We fool ourselves more than we think, but it doesn't matter. What's important is to see the difference between pure enthusiasm and self-involved excitement. This is lot easier to do when we can see signals outside as well as in."

"You know," Harley said, "this is a big issue with me. I'm still surprised sometimes by the way people open up to my suggestions. I'm afraid I'll miss my self involvement and end up hurting someone."

"Me too. I really want to see myself more clearly, and it's a help to know that when I *am* self involved, others will pick it up even if I don't. But you know, there is one thing I've noticed. It's absolutely impossible to be self-involved when I'm really centered. Now if only it were possible to be centered all the time."

"It is. Look at Yew."

Staring at the cold tea sitting in their cups, each of them smiled. Harley rose silently and glided through the inner door to his office.

Mel sat a while, then started home. She strolled quietly in the cool evening air, simply enjoying the peace and Clarity in the deepening night sky.

She was startled to see Yew waiting as she reached her usual path.

"I felt like talking this evening," he said, anticipating her question. "Mind if I join you?"

"Of course not," Mel beamed back.

As they walked, Yew slid a picture into Mel's hand. It showed a cold and barren world faintly lit by a distant star.

"What is it?" she asked.

"It's a computer generated image of a planet that once held life. The star isn't distant. It's dying. How does it make you feel?" he asked softly.

"Kind of sad," she returned. "But it's really interesting to see the way the universe comes and goes. What planet is it?"

"Earth. Not for a long time, but it's coming."

She shuddered as a cold wave swept through her stomach.

"It brings it home, doesn't it?" he said gently. "But why do you suppose it hit so hard? We'll be long gone when the sun dies."

Mel stopped walking and took a long breath, relaxing as she exhaled. After a few moments she began, her voice still tense, "I really can't say. But I don't see the point in dwelling on it."

"There isn't any point in dwelling on it. But there isn't any future in running from it either. There really is something to be gotten from looking at it for a moment."

"I knew I'd be in trouble if I said that," she smiled as she resumed her stroll. "So I'm ready. What am I supposed to get?"

"What do you get from your meditating?" he asked.

Surprised, she stopped again to think. "It makes me feel good. Whole and happy, I guess."

"Anything else?"

"Yes, I guess so. I feel peaceful, and the Clarity! There's no way I could do what I have to do without it. My creativity and competence both depend on it."

Yew looked deeply into her eyes as he talked. "That's all wonderful, but it's not enough."

Taken aback, Mel blurted, "What do you mean? It's enough for me! I'd say a peaceful, self-actualizing existence filled with creative competence isn't all that bad."

"Look at the picture again," he returned. "And remember what you're looking at."

Mel stared hard at the picture. Gradually her gaze softened, and she turned again to Yew. "What point is there in anything if it all just blooms to die? And don't say it's just a preparation for a new universe to be born. That doesn't make it meaningful for the universe we're in now."

"That's exactly what you should see. It's the point of the picture. Even the treasures you've been given through your meditating are pointless in the end. But there's more."

"What do you mean?"

"The real treasure waiting to be discovered through meditation isn't just happiness and peace and enhanced

75

creativity, as wonderful as these are. The real treasure is enlightenment. Enlightenment is the one treasure that will make sense of the universe as it really is in its entirety. Including its impermanence.

We can see the purpose and beauty in the natural cycles shorter than our own, because we see the continuity of the whole in the unity of our own existence. But when the cycle is longer than our own, it gets tough. Enlightenment gives us a much longer eye.

I'm not asking you to believe this now, without your own experience. But it's important to be open to this as a possibility, because meditating pushes us to give things an honest look, and this is our only hope of finding meaning and peace in the whole picture. If we have the courage to look deeply at things, the short answers just aren't enough.

You don't have to take my word for this. Just look for yourself. It's not quick and it's not easy. But over time your purification will open you to seeing past your fear, and the picture will not be troubling. And... Your goals will change."

Yew was already moving away as he finished. With a smile, he disappeared.

Mel walked a while longer, eventually turning toward the closet.

"Why not spend the night there?" she thought with a rush of inspiration.

She mounted the stairs with growing anticipation. Settling into her pillow on the floor, she slipped immediately into meditation.

Unexpectedly she soon saw her mind wandering, keeping track of how well she was doing. The worse she did, the more she kept track. And the more she kept track, the worse she did.

"Enough!" The word hissed into the air as she leapt to her feet. By the time she rejoined the night air she was becoming quiet. But her mind was troubled.

"Why does this happen now? It felt so right."

Then she began feel Clarity seeping into her mind. As she strolled she relaxed, and the Clarity seemed to fill the space opened by her relaxing.

"Pride," she said aloud. "I was more and more involved in my success instead of my relief as I sat there. My pride just took a form I hadn't noticed before so it could take control of my mind before I recognized it."

Relieved, she turned back to the closet. "Things will go differently now," she beamed with pride.

The night passed slowly. Try as she might, Mel couldn't steady her mind. Finally, sunken eyed and defeated, she faced the dawn.

Staring flatly out the window, she saw the sun touch the first color of Fall, silently bringing it to life. Mel's shoulders sagged and smile ran across her face as she watched her hidden tension dissolve.

Without turning, she knew Yew had slipped into the room. "Did I hear him?" she wondered. "I'm sure it's him."

Settling quietly next to her, Yew said nothing for a while. When he began, Mel felt her body relax more.

"It wasn't just your body that was tense. Your mind was active, so it was tense too. And your heart was heavy, which means it was dense and hard.

It's not easy to see which tension begins first, but it doesn't really matter. Heart, mind, and body all feed together. So if we change the diet for one we change it for them all. Enthusiasm always helps. This is a big part of the secret of a happy life, and it's what you found outside the window just now. You know, you wouldn't have found it if you had expected it to be there."

Mel's mind churned as she faced Yew blankly. "Does he really expect this to make sense?"

Yew smiled through his soft drawl. "You really do know what I'm talking about. You just spent a long night trying to meditate without any luck. Then the moment the dawn lit the trees your heart melted. It took you by surprise. It wouldn't have worked so well if you had expected it."

"Why not?" She was trembling.

Yew continued, "It doesn't really matter. Lots of things can sweep us away and make us lose sight of what we really want. Sometimes a little surprise can bring us back on track. It's good to take a look when this happens. Mainly to learn how we open space for a miracle."

"Miracle?"

"Yes. The big one, when a negative feeling turns around. Your yearning is beginning to go on in the background even when things are not going well. Things begin to change more quickly when this happens. And your dreams are showing that your purification is beginning in earnest. This means that your practice is accelerating the positive as well as the negative unfolding of your karma. A mantra would help you now. Do you know what a mantra is?"

"Isn't it a series of sounds or words that people repeat over and over?"

"That's right, but do you have any idea what the point is?"

"No."

"A mantra is for protection. What do you suppose the mantra would be designed to protect?"

"Probably it would be meant to protect the mind."

"True, but against what?"

Mel paused. Finally she spoke, "Against negativity?"

"Yes, against pessimism and negativity. Together, they're like a living death. Repeated with devotion countless times, a mantra gradually fills the back of the mind with power and love, and that protects the mind from itself."

"Wouldn't any positive affirmation work the same way?"

"Yes. Any affirmation can work if it is repeated often enough with devotion, but the mantra also has the power of its own sound. When transmitted properly from a teacher, this power is magnified by its passage through many generations of purified hearts."

Yew paused the way he usually did before asking a question, so Mel was ready. "Why do you suppose spiritual unfoldment is called enlightenment?"

Mel replied immediately, "Partly because it sheds light on the nature of spirit. And partly because experience of light is so much a part of it, I suppose."

"Good. But there's more. A light heart is an essential part of freedom, not just because it frees us to see the silliness of our old cares. A heart becomes light and clear, less dense and dark, as it loses its hardness. There's more, too. Desire disappears. There is nothing hard, nothing solid, for the world to hook onto. It's not just that our desires are fulfilled. There's simply nothing - no grasping, no craving, no fear, no pride - for the world to hook onto."

"So there's just no room for negative feelings?"

"That's not quite it. A soft heart has infinite space. What happens is that nothing short of peace, bliss, and love has any appeal when we relax completely. Desires, even ones that have seemed very important, just aren't there any more. They can come if they wish, but they pass right through a completely open heart. There's nothing hard inside for them to hold onto. Love, on the other hand, needs no point of attachment. When we discover we're swimming in an ocean of love we don't need to capture a handful and call it our own. Once the cosmic saturation of love is discovered we don't need to grab it for ourselves. We see it all around and through us. We realize we've been dying of thirst as we churned in a sea of nectar. Our exertions and fears just kept us from noticing."

"So we stop swimming and just float instead," Mel beamed effortlessly.

He looked at her. "Yes." He knew she knew. And he knew she was ready.

Chapter 8

Growing Pains

Days had passed quickly with a lightness Mel had never known, but this had gradually been lost to a growing darkness in her nights.

"Why is this happening to me?" she thought feverishly. Recalling the few vivid nightmares from her childhood, her experience of the past few nights had been worse. There was something darker and more sinister about these dreams. The bears in her dreams were mauling more than just her body.

Yew had looked at her strangely yesterday.

"I'm sure he knows what is going on," she murmured. "What did he mean when he said the water in the glass was being stirred? Maybe I should have talked about it, but he should have pushed me harder if he thought I needed help. Why did I just look away?"

Bounding from her bed, she heard herself say, "This time will be different."

Within moments she was moving through the morning air to find her teacher.

She found him waiting on the bench under the Old Oak. Dawn was just breaking as she walked breathlessly up to his still form. Sitting, she knew he was waiting for her to become quiet before he would begin.

Taking a long breath, she felt filled with love and a peculiar kind of security. It was hard to tell if it was coming from Yew or from deep within her own heart, but she felt a warmth and steadiness overtake her, just as she had felt in the folds of her mother's arms.

"The steadiness of the rocking chair," she thought. "That's what mother meant. She must have known... Steadiness doesn't come from rigidity, it comes from quiet balance."

She turned to Yew. She would be able to see now.

His eyes were waiting for hers. As they met, the feeling of warmth increased.

Finally he spoke, "Your dreams are a good sign. They show you're becoming purified."

"It doesn't seem that way while I'm dreaming," she returned flatly.

"You need to understand what it means to stir the water in the glass," Yew said quietly. "Imagine the mind as a glass of muddy water. When we want peace and Clarity we pause and let the mud settle to the bottom. This is part of the gift that comes through meditating. The quiet opens us to Clarity and inspiration. But we still need to purify mind. Otherwise any little disturbance of the world will stir up the mud again. And this usually happens when we need Clarity the most. So we learn to watch quietly as the world stirs the water in the glass. If we're quiet we can see what's going on without becoming involved in self-judgment. This is very hard to do, but it's not impossible. And when we persist, purification gradually comes along as a matter of course."

"Like in psychoanalysis?"

"Not exactly. We dig in a different way, and we aim for much more than fellowship with normal human misery. Psychoanalysis can be very helpful, but we have to see it just as a beginning. Our practice centers on the present, not the past.

Over time we become aware of exactly what is operating through every action of our lives. Purification depends on this kind of awareness. This enables us to let things unfold naturally."

Mel felt a mixture of remorse and indignation as she shot back, "So my dreams mean I've been doing things all wrong?"

"Absolutely not," Yew said. "Growth and purification frequently are painful even when they needn't be. The important thing is that when they are painful we need to move immediately to shelter our focus and resolve. Adversity always brings good, as long as we can survive it with our peace and Clarity intact."

"Okay, but show me how these dreams are supposed to bring me good. What am I getting from them that I couldn't get another way?" Her voice was strained.

"It doesn't really matter if there are other ways for you to grow. The other ways could be just as painful. The problem isn't the process of growth. The problem is that you are hanging on with one hand to what your other hand is trying to release."

Mel recoiled, "So the bears I'm dreaming about are my own fault? Why would I wait until now to do this to myself? I wasn't having problems before, and I don't see any change in my practices."

"No. The bears are not your fault, even if they come in response to your own mind."

Before Mel could respond, he continued, "The bears are your mind's reaction to your attempts to subdue it. You've been working to assert control of your mind, and it simply doesn't want you to succeed. Your inspiration was enough to carry you for a while, but this has been blunted a little by the passing of time. So you have less going for you just when you need all the help you can get. Your mind is taking you seriously now, and it is fighting as hard as it can to keep you from becoming its master."

Mel was quiet now. "How can I beat it? The bears in my dreams are so much stronger than I am."

"It doesn't matter. You can win if you want, but you don't need to. You don't have to win the battle your mind is putting you in the middle of. Try to win the war instead. You do that through your practice of purification. The battle is just a game. Your mind picks a fight with you and you react by defending exactly what you're trying to get rid of. It picks a fight where, win or lose, it is the winner. If it wins, you've lost your battle to control your mind. If it loses, all you've done is preserve your pride, which is the source of your fear. Look at what you're worried about in the battle. What do you really have to lose to the bears?"

Mel started to answer, then fell silent. Finally she spoke slowly, "At first it seemed like I was protecting my life. But the bears never kill me. Sometimes I wish they would, just to be done with it."

Yew said nothing as she paused.

Finally she continued, "In the end, I guess my pride is all I'm really protecting, and that's not me."

"That's exactly right, but how did you get there?" he asked.

Mel smiled, "First I remembered the relationship between fear and pride. So I realized my fear in the dreams had to be coming from my ego somehow. But this didn't help me much. All it did was make me feel frustrated and guilty. Then I noticed that this was exactly what happens whenever my pride makes me vulnerable to negativity. And suddenly I felt free. My negativity isn't me. I saw that my pride, the impurity in my ego, is the problem.

I saw myself identifying with my threatened pride, as though it was really *me*. I saw how my pride pushes me to defend it before I have a chance to think about what I'm really doing, what I'm really protecting. In the end I saw how I end up protecting the source of my own misery. And the funny thing is that when I realized this, I didn't feel frustrated. Just free."

The sun was beginning to warm the morning air.

"What should I do now?" she asked, settling into the bench.

"You want purification, so why not just look at everything in terms of this goal. This means we don't look at what we ought to be doing. We look at how we ought to be doing it."

"So it doesn't matter what I do. Just how I do it."

"Not quite. It does matter what we do. That's one of the reasons why we focus on how we do it."

"This doesn't make sense," she said. "It sounds like double talk. How I do something comes second. What I do comes first. You just turned things around so that the cause follows the effect. How am I supposed to understand this?"

Yew smiled, "It really does make sense. If we look carefully we can see that how we do things plays a big part in choosing what we do. I'm not talking about how proficiently we do something. Think in terms of the process we use to do everything we do, especially how we make decisions about what we're going to do. What's important is that we let all of our mental and physical acts emerge quietly. This helps because enthusiasm bonds with love when we're quiet, and when this happens everything simply goes better. Even our decisions about what we want to do are clearer and better. Remember when we talked about the secret of a happy life? We were talking about enthusiasm, but that's just part of it. The secret of a happy life is to have enthusiasm coupled with love."

Mel felt her lungs relax into emptiness. "I think I understand," she said. Then she felt tension refilling her as she continued, "But how do we get to this point? It seems like another closed circle. We control mind naturally when quiet enthusiasm and love come together. But so what? When mind is quiet it's natural for it to be well behaved. So when I have the chicken I have the egg, and when I have the egg I have the chicken. But when I don't have either, how do I get in?"

"It's not a chicken and egg thing at all. We can find enthusiasm and love through our purification practices. They open us to grace, mostly by changing what we really want. Purification is important because it removes obstacles. We generally find the biggest obstacle is our own resistance to grace. Over time we can chip away at this resistance until we're able to surrender.

This is a practical approach. We start by filling our mind with the right things. This is easier when we surround ourselves with peaceful people and places, so we do this as much as we can.

Everyone knows lots of ways that don't work when we try to control our mind. It isn't easy to look past the games and settle into what is important. Our pride hooks us and forces us to play the games that are thrown at us. The trick is to purify our habits and our ego until we can keep sight of our real goals even when the world seeks to involve us in gaming. And we can do this systematically.

Even when we're able to see through the games, we're not finished. Actual mastery of mind depends on a continuing purification. We have to become gentle with ourselves. There's no way to master the mind by force. We just have to quiet down. Mastery of mind comes from relaxing our grip, not flexing it. No one can do this alone. It takes Grace, and that can come through a teacher or directly from God. But either way we have to become able to accept it, and purification is a direct route to that."

Mel stood and walked into the sun. It warmed her back gently as she turned to Yew. "Okay. Now I see why I'm having bad dreams and how important purification is, but what do I do to get some rest? It's wonderful to talk about all this in the warm morning sun beneath the Old Oak, but I need some relief tonight when I'm miserable."

Yew smiled. "It's a good sign that you're taking this seriously, but you have to avoid giving it more power by reacting in fear. Not many dreams are really important, and the ones that are important usually have a symbolic nature. Dying in a dream, for instance, can be a wonderful thing if we understand what the death symbolizes. Remembering the symbolic nature of dreams can strip them of much of their negative power. And... Do you remember when I mentioned lucid dreaming?"

"Yes, but I don't really understand it. I assume it refers to the ability to bring our waking awareness into our dream experiences," she answered. "It's been happening more and more."

"Good," he said. "You need to focus on this now more than ever."

"How?"

"You can begin while you're awake by telling yourself that you're really dreaming. This helps sometimes. After many repetitions, the thought becomes automatic, springing forth by habit. It can even enter your mind while you're busy dreaming. After all, it's the same mind whether we're asleep or awake.

How we enter sleep affects our dreams too. It's helpful to quiet down before retiring. And it helps to do something uplifting. It is difficult to watch the news without becoming disquieted, and this may interfere with sleep. There's no point in giving yourself a load of fresh activity to deal with when you have enough old stuff to contend with already. Studying scripture or meditating can leave you prepared for sleep with a quiet mind. This will lighten your load, and it will open a memory of your desire for awareness as you drift into sleep. You'll enter sleep with increased focus and protection."

"Protection?"

"Yes. Scriptural study and meditation open us to love and grace. Protection is part of this grace. In time, love can come to fill our entire being. When this happens we truly are one with the Infinite. There's no greater source of protection. Until then we need all the help we can get."

Yew stood and moved away. "We can talk more tomorrow if you want."

Mel lingered a while and enjoyed the sun.

Chapter 9

Dawn

"Who would have expected?" Mel thought as she hurried through the morning gloom. It had been a long night.

She found Yew as he had been the day before, sitting quietly on the bench under the Old Oak. Her heart pounded as she settled next to him. He smiled as he turned toward her. She often wondered at that smile. Then she noticed her pulse had quit its pounding.

Apparently satisfied, he nodded for her to begin.

"After what you said yesterday, last night started really well. I meditated for a while, then reminded myself to be aware while I slept. I was ready for the bears, but they never came. What happened was much worse. I dreamed I was standing on a cedar hummock in a small clearing deep in a woods. I was enjoying the color and softness of the earth. I bent to take some in my hand when a snake suddenly lunged at me from nowhere. I grabbed it before it bit me, but I just wasn't strong enough to protect myself. Eventually it bit me in the chest. Then it just slithered away. I woke up immediately and couldn't get back to sleep all night."

Yew's voice was sober. "How did you feel when this was happening?"

Mel's voice trembled. "Mostly astonished. Scared too, I guess. But I think I was more scared after I woke up than I was in the dream. I think it just happened too fast."

"It doesn't take long to be scared," Yew smiled. "This is a good sign. But the snake shows some difficulty is coming into your life very soon."

Mel looked at Yew incredulously. "Are you saying this dream is precognitive? I can't believe that."

"Fine. It's better to disbelieve until we experience for ourselves. I'd be more concerned if you were too suggestible. Then you might actually bring negative activity into your life by your gullibility. But it's still a good idea to plan ahead a little extra right now. You may have a few days before things become challenging, but it's hard to say. Don't worry though. It's not going to threaten your life. Your response in the dream speaks to that. But you will have to put all your energy into your own affairs for a short time.

Mel felt her eyes tensing. "I have to quiet down," she thought as she drew in a long quiet breath. She noticed Yew was doing the same. Mel smiled as she settled into the familiar warmth.

Eventually she noticed her eyes were closed. Opening them, she saw the sun creeping toward her spot on the bench. Yew was still with her, watching silently.

When he withdrew his eyes, she felt the morning breeze for the first time and she wondered, "Was he sheltering me somehow?"

"The breeze was touching you all the time," he began. "But only on the outside. You were sheltered inwardly. Try to remember this through the next few days. The world may touch us outwardly, but our inner experience is what's important. This is where we really are. What happens in our outer world is good or bad for us only in terms of how we respond to it inwardly. If it pushes us toward truth, peace and Clarity, it is good. If it pushes us away, then it's bad. And we're more in charge of this than it sometimes seems. Eventually, through practice and grace, we can accept everything as a wake up call to push us toward freedom. Until then, we need protection. Shelter yourself from unnecessary activity for a while. Things will work out fine. Just remember to remember."

Yew stood up, smiled, and left.

Mel watched him disappear down the trail, then walked quietly to her office and got to work. By the end of the day her schedule had been cleared for the rest of the week. "Why not?" she had said. "I've never taken any time off. I think I'm due." No one had argued.

Walking home, Mel felt a wash of peace as the twilight deepened. It was a strange sort of security.

"The rocker," she murmured.

**

Morning dawned and Mel awakened slowly. Gradually she remembered her night. No dreams. Just a long deep sleep. Stretching, she felt wonderful. Rolling from her bed, she felt her smile widen as she stepped lightly onto the floor.

Before her first step was finished, she felt a sharp stab of pain deep in her back. She watched her knees buckle as she headed for the floor. Catching herself as best she could, she braced for the pain.

"Breathe," she thought furiously as she groped for a comfortable position. Gradually she bent into her knees and the pain subsided. But she couldn't move. The slightest tensing of her back shot fresh pain through her body.

It felt odd when she began to smile, but she couldn't help herself. "At least I don't have worry any more about what's going to happen. But why this? There's never been anything wrong with my back before. All I did was step out of bed!" She was interrupted by fresh pain.

"I have to relax. The pain leaves when I'm still."

She began with a tiny breath, drawn so slowly she barely sensed the air flowing into her lungs. All the while, she focused on relaxing and pictured the face of her teacher. Gradually she began to feel his presence. Then, just as the pain dissolved into the familiar warmth she heard his voice. Distant at first, then gradually nearer. It took a while for Mel to realize that he actually was there.

Yew was whispering, "Don't talk, and don't move. Just breathe and yield to the relief. Your back hasn't been out long, so it will go back into place easily. But the muscles have to relax first. Yield to the feeling of relief and be mindful of your breath. Don't think about it. Just do what you have to do."

Mel felt a tingling sensation flowing beneath her skin through her entire body. Without hesitation, she yielded completely. Her pain dissolved into the bliss.

Gradually she noticed that she was in a peculiar posture on the floor. She knew she was alone, and she knew she could move without pain. Slowly unbending, it took a while for her to stand and get her bearings.

"I must have been down for quite a while. It's dusk already. I wonder if Yew is still here somewhere."

She stopped short as she heard the familiar morning birds begin to sing. She reached the window just in time to see dawn break on a cloudless day.

"Tomorrow? How could I have been on the floor so long? This isn't possible."

Turning toward the door, she felt her knees buckle. She flinched against a pain that never came.

"What's happening?" she thought as she felt the floor ridges in her knees.

She walked gingerly to the outside door. It was locked.

"I thought so. How on Earth did Yew get in?"

She walked to her window. Locked. By this time her feet were flying. Checking each window and door, she quickly discovered that it was impossible for anyone else to have been inside.

"It gets stranger and stranger," she said as she threw on her clothes. Within seconds she was on the trail.

Skipping through the clear morning air, she found Yew sitting on their bench beneath the oak.

Slipping quietly next to him, she felt no urgency to talk. The air seemed alive with nourishment, and she drank deeply as she breathed, remembering for the first time that she had been a day without food.

Eventually Yew turned to her. "It's probably a good idea to bring me up to date before you ask anything."

Mel was perplexed. "Don't you already know what happened?"

"Not really," he replied. "I only know that you weren't here yesterday and that the most important thing for me to do was to support you in my heart. It was clear from your dream that you were about to face a challenge. But it also was clear that you were up to facing it on your own, and it didn't seem wise to interfere. Opportunities are easily ruined by interference."

"But you were there with me. Didn't you feel this too?"

"Not the way you felt it."

Watching Mel's shoulders sag, he continued, "This doesn't mean it wasn't real. It just means you touched me very deeply, on the causal level. Tell me what happened."

Mel quickly told her tale, ending with a question. "Why was I in that odd position when I woke up?"

"In the first place, you have to believe that you weren't asleep. You were meditating, and you were experiencing what is called samadhi. While you were in this state your body was moved into a posture called an asana. Asanas are part of the discipline of yoga, so they're quite natural. Sometimes they emerge spontaneously through meditation. When your back was relaxed, your body was moved to assume the posture that would allow it to slip back into place. Then the muscles were healed by the natural energy that fills the sanctuary of samadhi.

This healing energy has more than one name. An acupuncturist would call it Chi. This is the energy that healed you through your samadhi experience. But the important thing isn't the experience. The real gift is your realization of the way things really are. This gives you inspiration, faith, and freedom from fear. Courage isn't important when we realize we have nothing to fear."

"Does this mean I'm actually finished?" Mel asked.

"Not exactly," Yew replied. "But it does mean that you're actually beginning."

Chapter 10

Young Pride and Old Confusion

Time had passed quickly. Now Mel suddenly found herself staring blankly across her desk at the hard face of Jason Alteridge. Dumb with shock and amazement, her words fell awkwardly from her mouth. "I have no problem changing absolutely any aspect of the structure or focus of this project," she began, "but nothing at all is going to happen until I have some time to think about this. I'll be in touch within a week. I trust you can wait until then."

A chill swept through her as she watched Jason silently rise and leave. This was her first contact with Jason in weeks, but she couldn't imagine how so much could have changed. Their last words had been pleasant, even if a little more distant than she had expected. Without thinking, she reached for the buzzer to Harley's office. Within seconds, he slid quietly through the inner door, a look of concern on his face. The buzzer was seldom used, and this was hardly the time he would have expected it. Seeing Mel he stopped short, easing gently into the chair across from her.

Mel finally stood and moved toward the door. "Jason wants our jobs. He says his father will pressure the board to dismantle the project unless he's put in charge. We have to see Yew." Harley trotted behind.

They passed silently until they could see Yew sitting under the Old Oak. Before they could begin, he said quietly, "I see I'm about to discover why I came to work early this afternoon. I'm sure you're facing a real challenge, but please try to look at it as an opportunity. The important thing is to keep looking for meaning. Let's talk in the closet."

Mel felt her spirits lift as they walked together. "Why is it," she thought, "that my happiness and peace of mind are vulnerable to Jason's treachery? I DON'T NEED THIS!"

She noticed Yew and Harley were staring at her, paused on the steps. "Oh," she blurted, "I didn't realize I was talking out loud."

"You weren't," Yew said, "but you weren't walking either."

"You may find," he continued as they reached the closet, "that your disquiet is resolved when you understand your experience just now on the stairs."

"You mean when I thought I had been talking? I don't see how that's going to help me." Mel settled into her usual spot on the carpet, muttering, "Jason is the problem. Some artist he turned out to be."

"The point is, you didn't see what was going on just now on the stairs. You were so wrapped up in your feelings that you didn't see what was happening around you. This isn't a little thing. It may not be a big deal when it happens like that on the stairs, but it happens in bigger ways too. Like when you let Jason fool you. And even this is only a symptom of a bigger problem. Not just for you. It's a problem for everyone. How can we trust our judgments? How can we tell when our inspiration is misled by our involvement?

Let's look at Jason. Jason is a problem because he's being centered on himself. But do you really think his actions are unusual?"

"I thought he was supposed to be an artist," Mel said. "Some artist. How can he be an artist when he's so self-involved?"

"Lots of successful artists are self-involved. Have all the great intuitive geniuses in human history been wonderful people? Try to relax and see that the issue here isn't with Jason. What he's doing, or even how well he's doing it, isn't all that important. What's important is to know how to tell our pure and true inspirations from the ones clouded by our projections.

Jason might be completely unaware of his involvement. If he looks, he might only see anger or frustration, just as you would see in yourself if you looked right now. If we're trying to root out our projections from among our true inspirations, we have to look for their source. To do this, we look for signals that ego is infiltrating our responses. And anger is as strong a signal as we're likely to find."

"Fine," Mel murmured toward the floor, "but I wasn't angry while Jason was manipulating me for the past year."

"Perhaps not," Yew responded gently, "but if you look deeply enough you may find other signals still suggesting you were being moved by your ego. And if you keep looking, you may find that your ego was being moved by Jason."

Mel thought about this for a moment before replying, "I guess so. But how could he have fooled me so completely? I feel awful. Everything I believe is based on my faith that the flow of inspiration which brings me my peace, my intuition, and my compassion, is a flow of goodness."

Mel watched her voice get louder as she continued, "You said my intuition was the source of truth, my access to real Mind. It sure doesn't look that way now. How could Jason have fooled me? Now one of my closest and most intuitively gifted friends is turning out to be my worst enemy. Right now my cancer isn't the problem, he is!"

"He sure is," Yew said as he quietly settled onto the soft floor, "but his ego is as poisonous to him as it is to you.

I know this is hard to see, but ego can be either our best friend or our worst enemy. Even though the courage and resolve of a strong ego are essential to persevering on a path toward enlightenment, ego eventually comes to be our most powerful enemy. It keeps us from moving on. It gets us moving and sustains us through difficulties, but in the end it can blind us to the truth we've been working to uncover. It makes us see what we want to see instead of permitting us to see truth simply as it's given.

This is perfectly normal. Unpurified ego is the natural fruit of ordinary actions, and it's just preserving itself. It lives on our involvement, and it compels our involvement through fear and deception. We're compelled to protect it because we're deceived into believing it is our essence. But things don't have to be this way.

Look at what goes on. There's not a lot that ego and intellect can do well. We've all seen what happens when they interfere with things we normally do comfortably. We can lose our ability to function smoothly by thinking intellectually about what we're doing, especially when ego hooks us with its concerns. But ego doesn't have to be our enemy. It has the power to keep us going sometimes when we're discouraged. And even though it can isolate us from truth and peace, it also can empower us to accept grace."

Mel started, facing Yew as she spoke, "This is beginning to make sense. Until the other evening I thought I was my ego. Since then though, it's been obvious that it really is external, something pushing me back and forth. So it finally makes sense to think in terms of letting it go."

"That's important," Yew continued. "It's hard to see the assumptions that lie beneath our beliefs, but we have to root them out if we're serious about enlightenment. We can't hope to find truly new ground if we allow any constraints at all on our vision. It's especially hard to see the workings of our own egos, but we need to do this or we can't have faith in our feelings. This is one of the most important things we have to do, and it seems that you're being helped with it right now."

Yew paused while Mel and Harley slid to the floor. After a few moments he began to talk again, "Let's just relax for a while and become Young. Take a few breaths and let go of our past experience."

A peculiar feeling overtook the friends as the room settled into quiet. They would never be sure if Yew was talking or if they were experiencing what he was feeling without words. But the warmth was familiar as they drifted together into a New World.

Enveloped by a strangely reassuring darkness, they knew they were in a large chamber within a vast cave. Gradually they became part of a world where light seems as dark, and dark seems as light, but their awareness of this dimmed as they moved into the life of Young.

> *Young awakened and watched the play of shadows on the wall. Her sleep cycles were shorter than most, so she enjoyed regular moments to herself. Then she noticed the feeling. It wasn't the feeling she wanted, but it had become a regular part of her moments of solitude. She knew what would follow. "Why can't I just enjoy the shadows?" she thought as her legs unfolded. "Why do I have to feel so driven?"*

> *Young watched herself rise and turn from the Great Wall. The turmoil in her stomach eased as she faced the blackness of the void that*

surrounded her on three sides. "This time I guess I'll do it," she said to herself as she cautiously stepped away from her past.

For the first time in her memory, Young didn't compete in the Shadow Games. They were just finishing when she eased back into sight.

One of her friends was the first to see her. Rushing to her, Jamie panted in her eager way, "Where have you been? We've all been really worried. Are you okay? I know you're disappointed, but don't worry. You can take back your championship at the next game."

Jamie was a kind person, but she wasn't inclined to notice what was going on while she was talking. So she didn't notice Young's face until she paused to breathe, blurting, "Oh! What's happened?"

"You won't believe!" Young beamed back. "I've just been beyond the light of the fire."

Jamie was speechless. Finally she stammered, "Who are you going to tell? You know everyone will think you're crazy."

Young just smiled and turned a weary head toward her bed.

After a short but sound sleep, Young awakened to find a pensive Jamie sitting quietly by her bed. "What's wrong?" Young began. "Are you okay?"

"I just wanted to talk," Jamie replied in an uncharacteristically quiet way. "You know, I

think a lot about the games everyone plays, and I don't really have anyone who I can talk with about this. But if you've been beyond the light of the fire, then you must think a lot about this too."

"I don't know if I think a lot about it," Young returned as she stretched to her feet, *"but I do have a lot of feelings that don't fit with what everyone else wants me to believe."*

"Like what?" Jamie asked eagerly in her normal voice.

Young took a long breath, relaxing as she began, *"It just seems strange to me that everyone would place so much value on the shadows. What good are the games if they aren't for the benefit of the people who play them? But if this is true, if the players are more important than the game, then why doesn't it seem this way when people are playing? It gets harder and harder for me to compete. I see the light playing on my opponents, the way it highlights their features and illumines their feelings. I have more and more trouble concentrating on the shadows when this happens. I find myself actually asking why darkness should be more sacred than light?"*

As soon as Young had said this, Jamie's mouth began to move, but she was stopped before the words could flow.

"I know what you're going to say," Young drove on. *"Of course I know the light is sacred. And I know we're measured against it. But don't you see? We're measured by the artistic*

darkness we cast with our shadows against the great wall. We make our mark. But what's the point?"

Young paused, her tone softening a little as she watched Jamie's face slacken in despair.

"I'm not saying the games are bad," she continued, "and I'm not saying they're good. The games are neutral. We can compete fairly or unfairly. The point is that I don't see any meaning in them."

Jamie's voice rang, "So you're trying to make sense of things by turning all of our values inside out?"

"I'm not trying to do anything," Young went on. "All I'm saying is that I think the players are more important than the game. And that I see beauty and value in the truth that emerges directly from the light of the fire, not in our power or our shadows."

Both friends sat silently for a while. Finally Jamie rose, saying, "This makes a lot of sense to me. I just wonder how many others are uncomfortable with what we've been taught. I'm going to talk to a few of my friends. Will you be here for a while?"

"Sure," Young replied as she stood, "I still have to eat breakfast, even though it's probably supper time for you. But I imagine I'll be trying to work up the courage to take a real trek soon."

Young watched as Jamie skipped off. "I'd better eat quickly," she thought to herself. "The way she's moving, she may not be gone long."

As it turned out, Young was right. Jamie returned with several friends before Young had finished her breakfast. All were bubbling with enthusiasm, which they politely subdued until Young had hurriedly finished the rest of her food.

As soon as Young had drawn a deep breath, Jamie started, "They can't believe you actually did it. They want to hear it from you."

Young flushed a little as she began as evenly as possible, "All I did was walk two steps beyond the perimeter of light. Then I turned around and came home."

"But how did you find your way?" Jamie asked a little proudly, feeling herself to be the spokesperson of the group.

"I just turned toward the sacred fire," Young explained. "I know we've been taught that this is impossible, but really the fire can be seen from beyond the perimeter it actually illuminates."

"So you really stepped into the dark and didn't fall into the void?" Jamie continued as questioner.

"I didn't find any void," Young went on. "I know as well as you what we've been taught. All I can say is that I went beyond the perimeter of light and found the same ground there as here."

"What are you going to do next?" her questioner continued.

Young's eyes flashed as she said quietly, "Go farther."

Jamie's voice became sober, "What makes you think you have the right?"

"Young drew a long deep breath, quieting her pounding pulse a little before she continued, "I don't know. All I know is that it feels right to explore. What is the point in all of this if we aren't exploring to find truth? That's the only meaning I can find in my life."

"But what makes you think you won't be punished?" Jamie pressed.

"Faith," Young replied. "Maybe it's just faith in coherence. I don't know. But if I think calmly and evenly, it only makes sense when I think human being has value. I can't say why. But it doesn't matter. If there's no value in human being, then I'm not risking much. And if there is value in my existence, then my growth must increase that value. And too, if the universe is coherent it must be fair. And if this is true, then innocent and deep questioning can't be wrong. So I guess I just believe I have a birthright as a human being to explore."

What happened next was not what Young expected. No one said a word. After a moment of complete silence, everyone just started applauding. As one, all of her friends applauded. Young felt her spirit strengthen, buoyed by the enthusiasm and support of her friends.

Finally, when all was quiet once again, Jamie spoke quietly, "It might be a good idea for us to keep this to ourselves. Probably the best help we can give Young is to make sure we don't cause her any problems. We can meet our need for talking about it by talking with each other. Anyone who wants to can move on over to my place. Then we'll have sympathetic ears when we need them."

There was a general murmur of approval before Young began, "Thanks. You know you've helped me, but you probably don't know how much." And with that, she turned and walked away from the light and security of her Old World.

As she walked, Young found herself thinking, "What am I after, really?"

And then she heard a word. Not the way one usually hears a word. The word came from inside her. But it wasn't just a thought. At least it wasn't a thought that seemed to come from her. She'd been having this experience more and more lately. This time it was just one word, "Truth."

"What does this mean?" she thought as she walked toward the perimeter of light. "What is truth, really, and how am I supposed to measure it? Not by conformity, the way they taught me. What good is truth that's measured just by its conformity to the rules of our belief system? And why would they have taught me to believe in this kind of truth?"

Thinking these kinds of thoughts, Young quickly reached the perimeter of firelight. Passing into the darkness, Young turned to find once again that she still could see the fire past the perimeter of its illumination. She knew she could use it to find her way back if she wished, even though it couldn't help her explore. She felt a thrill pass through her as she stepped carefully ahead, this time with a resolve strengthened by the support of her friends.

She passed fairly quickly through the blackness until she heard the sound of water. Cautiously approaching in the darkness, she reached the edge of what seemed to be a vast and moving current of water, blocking her path away from the sacred fire. After pausing a while, Young returned again to share her discovery with her friends.

Much was made about the river, and Young's status within her small but trusted circle of friends was elevated as a result of her discovery. So before the end of that sleep cycle, Jamie persuaded Young to lead a small but courageous band of followers to the river. And as soon as all had rested, this is exactly what she did. Linking hands in the dark, they passed together to the lip of the water.

"Now that we're here," Young found herself saying, "I'm happy to lead you back if you wish, but the fire can lead you just as well. My plan is to cross the river. If anyone wishes to continue as well, they may, but we cannot go together. Clinging to one another we will sink, but I believe if we have the faith to relax enough the

water itself will support us as we paddle quietly along."

Quickly finding herself alone once again, Young watched the outline of the others recede against the image of the fire in the distance. Then she slipped into the warm water, feeling a thrill come and then subside as she relaxed and gently worked her way away from shore. After some time of this she began to tire, finally turning once again toward the light of the sacred fire to work gradually to shore. There she rested a while before returning by a new route home.

As she walked, she noticed that her feelings were different from the ones she'd had on her previous returns. Then she had been filled with the flush of victory. But this time she found herself calmly thinking as she trudged through the darkness toward home.

"The river is just too vast, too wide for me to cross," she mused. "Why don't I simply let it carry me where it will? Why do I have to limit my exploring by predetermining where I think it should lead? After all, the whole point of exploring is to discover the truth of reality without my expectations getting in the way. So next time we'll see where this river leads." Thinking this way, she returned unnoticed to rest in preparation for her next journey.

On awakening, Young moved immediately to prepare for a longer departure. Soon she was trotting lightly through the familiar darkness toward the river. Barely pausing at its bank, she slipped quietly into the warmth of its flow.

It didn't take long for her to pass the point where she felt she had been before. As she did, a keen sense of adventure overtook her, and she settled quietly into the bubbling progress of the river, thinking little of anything in particular. As she floated, alive in the presence of the moment, she was vaguely aware of the point of light fading gradually in the distance, but she felt no concern. Then she felt herself slow, her feet touching the bottom directly ahead. The current paused, but she could feel the flow continuing around her. "An island," she thought to herself. "But which way should I go? The safest way is to keep within sight of the sacred fire." So thinking, she pushed herself to the right and merged once again with the flow.

After a while she became aware of a sound. It was the sound of water. Lots of water. Falling with an unmistakable roar. And the current was accelerating. For a brief moment she paused in exhilaration, then decided to move as quickly as possible to shore. Looking to the light, she discovered that it was gone.

"How can I find my way to shore if I don't have my bearings?" she thought as she tried desperately to reestablish her orientation. Then she felt herself turning spontaneously to swim across the current. "Of course!" she thought. "If I entered the water with the flow over my left shoulder, then I exit with the flow coming from my right!"

It was not long, although it seemed a while in her worry, before Young reached the shore. As it turned out, this was none too soon. Mist from the waterfall gently sprayed her as she heaved herself onto the bank, flopping onto her back and barely noticing as she faded into a deep and untroubled sleep.

Awakening without stretching, Young quickly became oriented. "I know how to return, merely by walking with the river to my right until I see the light of the sacred fire, so I am in no danger here from my isolation. I may as well continue. But I know now that I must be vigilant, even when I feel secure in the flow. But this troubles me deeply. I felt so secure so long as I just floated along. I feel as though my faith has been violated. How can I trust my feelings when they just led me into such peril?" And then she remembered.

"The island! Why did I push toward home? I felt it was in order to be safe, to be sensible. But how can my home by the sacred fire help me when I am on my path of discovery? I must have erred by not allowing myself to detach from my old source of security."

And so Young began slowly to walk back upstream. When she reached the point by the river where the sacred fire was distantly visible as it had been at the island, she pushed off into the water and swam deliberately across until she reached land. Walking to shore, she continued upstream until she felt the shore bend to the right. Turning, it took little time to reach the next bend. Passing around it, she paused to take a last look at the distant glimmer of the sacred fire. And she saw something she had missed. Not the sort of something that she expected to see. And not the sort of something that she could see with her eyes. She saw a little deeper into her motives, especially into the reason she hadn't turned away before.

She saw this because she couldn't walk. Try as she might, she simply couldn't take the first step around the corner of the island that would take her completely away from the view of the sacred fire. "Why is this?" she asked herself. "Is this such a big step? After so much isolation and danger, what difference does this make now?"

Sensing that she wasn't on the verge of any forward movement, and unwilling to turn back, Young sat resolutely on the spot. As she sat she began to see what she was missing. "I'm not afraid of going on. I'd rather perish on the spot than live the rest of my life in the ignorance of my Old World. Something else is at work here." And then it was clear.

"Of course," she laughed out loud, "I'm not afraid of permanently leaving my Old World of ignorance. I'm just afraid of not being able to share my experiences with my friends! But why would this hold me so? They love me. They'd all want me to continue."

And then she heard a word. "Pride."

"Of course," she thought. "Unseen, unheard, unbidden ego has attached me to the fruits of my exploration. I guess when you get

right down to it, ego is the only fruit of any action. So my best friend has finally become my biggest adversary. My ego involvement with my friends is a bigger peril than the waterfall. Now I have to decide what I really want."

And then she heard another word. Gliding to her feet, she began striding happily down the beach, listening as the word "freedom" rang over and over in her ears. She felt a smile sweep across her face and envelop her whole being as she sang her way down the beach. And as she slid back into the water, she noticed she was floating a little higher than before.

Young quickly learned how to relax even more as she floated along. And she noticed that her awareness did not decrease as she let go of the tension that remained in her body and mind. In fact, there was a remarkable increase in her awareness and consciousness as she floated along. Nothing seemed to enter into her mind unbidden as she drifted, and her uncluttered mind seemed to increase remarkably in power. Floating in this state, she realized much of truth.

After some time of this, she began to see a light. She was certain at first that it was the light of the sacred fire, but it soon became apparent that it was much whiter than any light she had seen before. Soon she was swept into her first experience of sunlight, as the river flowed from the cave into the full light of a summer day. Senses overwhelmed, she floated gently to shore and sat in a gentle breeze under a tree for a long afternoon and evening before moving at dusk to explore her New World.

Young spent many days exploring mountains and valleys, experiencing beauty and light she had never dreamed possible. Then one day she came upon an opening, a cave, into which her river of origin flowed. "I wonder," she thought to herself, "Would this take me back to my old home? But what does this matter? I certainly don't want to go back to the Old World of darkness again."

So she went on her way, but soon found herself returning. As time passed, she noticed herself returning to the cave more and more often. "Why do I come here?" she heard herself ask. "Do I want to turn my back on all I've discovered just on the chance that I might survive to describe this to my friends? What good is their admiration to me when I have all of this?"

It was many days, and many visits to the cave opening, before Young understood. "No. I don't need their admiration. But I do feel their pain. They're lost. They can't enjoy the shadows and they haven't discovered real light. I must at least try to give them a chance to discover the truth and beauty I've found. I know that despite what they might think, their real needs can't be met by any stories I might tell, but perhaps I can at least encourage them to strike out to see for themselves.

And so it came to pass that Young slipped into the water once again, this time heading from light into darkness. But this time with her New World within her.

After some time floating in the blackness, she began to see a pale yellow light in the distance. Swimming to her right, she stepped onto shore and began making her way through the darkness toward the familiar fire. On her return, she found her sleeping place occupied by Jamie. Young was unable to escape as her startled friend launched immediately from deep sleep to excited questions, awakening others who had been sleeping nearby. Soon the entire area was buzzing in the excitement of Young's return. As she sat, Young watched herself sink gradually into deep sleep in the midst of the excitement.

On awakening, Young found she was completely out of synch with the sleep schedules of the others. This was just as well. Since so many friends were sharing her quarters, this permitted her to sleep wherever she wished. But she noticed that she was out of synch with the feelings of the others as well. Young had expected to be alienated from everyone but her friends, but she soon became discouraged by even her closest friends' attachment to their exploration.

"Their lives revolve around games just as much as the others," she thought. "They just play different games. And they don't even see that they're playing them. Instead of competing to cast shadows, they compete to see who can share the most exciting experience away from the sacred flame. Most of them are more interested in praise than in discovery. I wonder

if anyone really is interested in realizing the truth they all say they believe is so important?"

It took many sleep cycles for Young to see the keen interest beneath the ego involvement of her friends, but this finally did happen. By this time, her sleep schedule had accommodated the norm, and she was relaxing more in her conversation. But she felt a growing impatience with many who prompted her with questions. Some came hoping to gain a feeling of prestige by association with her. Others tried to satisfy their desire for experience vicariously through her descriptions of the world she had discovered. Young soon found her stories getting shorter, focusing more on how to reach the world of light and less on what was to be found there. Eventually she found herself talking very little, reserving her energy for those with the deepest enthusiasm. "It's not that I care less," she thought to herself. "I just want to give my energy to the ones who actually will use it."

Of course this initially offended some who found themselves outside her immediate attentions, but even they were unable to escape the feeling of warmth and compassion they felt when they were with her. Young watched with surprise and delight as some of them actually became gentle and enthusiastic explorers.

As she watched this happen, Young also felt a growing concern. Many of her friends had slipped into the river, each alone with the encouragement of her success and suggestions. But none had returned. It seemed a long while before she was tearfully awakened by Jamie's wet nudge and the words, "Can I borrow my bed back?"

Things changed quickly from then. Other dripping friends returned and the movement toward truth gained momentum. Of course many people still preferred the security of the cave. And others simply were loathe to abandon the prestige they had earned at the shadow games, causing them to protect their social interests by ridiculing Young and her friends. But even though times weren't always easy, the small band of friends prospered and grew, their ranks swelled by many who just wanted to know how they could be so happy.

As time passed, many new friends came and went by the river. But Young stayed on, leaving for moments in the world of light less and less frequently. Her life was mainly spent simply encouraging her growing family of friends to focus on truth, happiness, and what was needed for freedom. And there was no doubt that the little world of the cave was less old for her quiet activity."

Gradually Mel and Harley became aware once again of the closet surrounding them.

Looking at Yew, Mel spoke quietly, "I feel much better, but I still don't understand completely how this helps me."

Yew said, "Look at what you're trying to do. You're trying to help others find freedom. Before you can do this you have to become free yourself. What's needed for enlightenment? One thing is for sure. We have to understand the mental turmoil that makes us flinch from purification, and there's no way we can do this without appeal to our intuition. Our factual understanding isn't enough. Without our creativity, our intuition, enlightenment is impossible. And we can't use our intuition if we can't trust it."

Mel looked at Yew, speaking softly, "I see the point, but how can I trust my intuition? Look at how easy it was for Jason to fool me. At least when I think rationally I can tell when things aren't true."

"Of course," Yew returned. "But that isn't enough when we're searching for reality. We've lived long enough to realize that reality doesn't always fit with our logical expectations. Logic only helps us deal with the depth we've already discovered. It doesn't help us when we're trying to get further inside.

You've known this for a long time. You use your empathy to know others from the inside. You don't want to understand just their words, you want to understand *them*."

Mel felt a cold wave surge into her stomach. She felt herself flinch as she forced herself to look straight into Yew's eyes.

"I know you try not to violate people's privacy," he went on. "It's a good thing for you that you're careful. Using your empathy to manipulate others would hurt you more than it would hurt them."

Mel relaxed as Yew continued, "It's irrational to study just the surface when we're trying to get to the bottom of things. If we can see inside, it makes more sense to look there first, looking at the outside after we've seen where it's coming from. Then we can understand it better. This is what you do when you use your empathy. You don't bother to think about it because it just works. This isn't irrational. It's very rational to use intuition instead of rationality to do a job that can't be done any other way. It would be silly and irrational for you to do otherwise."

Mel felt her inner voice respond, "This is the point of the dream. I have to learn how to trust my intuition, how to let it help me instead of getting me into trouble. I have to learn to see when ego creeps into my intuition. Jason is my waterfall."

Yew smiled. "Yes, and now you're at the island once again. It might be nice for both of you to sit a while with Young in the sand." He slid from the room as the closet settled into darkness.

Chapter 11

Stretch - Duty into Freedom

Several days had passed. Now Harley sat quietly, watching the door that led to Mel's office. The wood had just begun to color with the richness of morning light when he heard footsteps on the other side. "That must be her," he thought as he rose. "And it sounds like she's in a hurry. I guess I was right."

Mel swept through her room. She felt Harley's anticipation as she reached the inner door. Opening it just far enough to scan his room, she spoke gently, "I thought you'd be here. Let's go. Yew probably is waiting."

Harley spoke quietly as they trotted though the dawn, "Are you okay?"

Mel felt a tingle as her voice trailed off, "I'm fine, but I can't talk now or I won't remember."

Harley smiled faintly, taking a deep breath of clear morning air.

Arriving at the building, they found the door unlocked without a trace of Yew. Mel immediately began scaling the stairs to the closet. "I'll bet he's waiting upstairs," she said as Harley followed breathlessly behind.

And so he was. Barely pausing at the unlocked door, the two friends slid quietly into their customary spots on the floor next to the still form of their teacher. When they were settled, he began, "Before you talk, cycle through a few breaths. Don't feel rushed. If you're centered when you begin, you won't forget. Time isn't a factor in complete remembering."

The air in the room gradually settled into quiet as the friends became still. Finally Mel began, "I just had a long dream. I was very centered when I went to sleep, and I'd been thinking about how hard it still is for me to trust my judgment."

Mel settled against the soft wall behind her as she continued easily, "In my dream, I heard a voice. At first it was my own voice, then the dream took on a life of its own. But through the whole dream I knew I was dreaming, and I knew I was being given a gift that was meant to help me solve my problem."

Her voice became distant as she continued. "Here's what I heard."

> *"Why is this happening to me? I should have been able to get around this one. It just shouldn't matter now. I'm not a kid any more. Now I'm leaving the hall for the last time. It's just not fair."*
>
> *Thinking these thoughts, the angry little man walked out the door into the clear air and paused. Fall had just begun to edge the air with the crispness that brings color early to the mountains of the North. But this was lost to the little man as he boiled home. He was too lost in thoughts of his past to appreciate the present.*
>
> *His feelings continued their spin downward as he entered his house, throwing his instrument onto the sofa. "Why do I look so stupid to everyone? I ought to be able to do what I want with my life."*
>
> *These moods never lasted long, and they didn't come very often. This was a bad one though, nearly as bad as when he got kicked off*

the basketball team when he was just a little boy. A very little boy, unfortunately. He remembered his last day of practice as the worst day of his life. "Why did they have to put me up against the tallest guy on the team?" he brooded darkly. He hadn't thought about that day for years. He'd learned not to. He knew what would follow.

For a long while he relived the humiliation he'd felt, furiously trying to reach the ball in his opponents hand. "It wasn't enough that the guy was so tall he could just hold the ball out of reach. He had to make it absolutely as bad as he could. At the least he could have moved a little instead of just standing there casually with one hand up in the air, forcing me to jump after it like a fool."

And then he heard the word. "Stretch!" Over and over came the cry of his team mates, laughing until practice had to be suspended until he had left - for the last time. But the word had haunted him, hanging to his back like an ugly suit ever since.

Now we should realize that Stretch really was a nice little person. And he really was very smart. But his success never seemed to show this. It wasn't that he was lazy. In fact he worked very hard, but it seemed the harder he worked the worse he did.

In the course of his life he failed at many things. After failing miserably at basketball he failed academically. Not literally, mind you. He always passed his examinations. But he never *excelled the way he felt he should. And worst of all, his heroic exertions gained him a reputation as an **over** achiever.*

Fortunately Stretch never became bitter. Of course he was frustrated, but he never became hard and bitter. In fact, he had a genuinely kind disposition. Perhaps this is why his destiny involved true greatness.

So Stretch settled into life as a poor musician. With the string bass as his instrument of choice, his income was very limited. We have to remember that Stretch was a small person. Very small... Now it wasn't just that as a 4 1/2 foot tall man he had to overcome an unusual number of difficulties in order to become a virtuoso on the string bass. In addition to this, the rituals and props he required in order to see the conductor and reach both ends of the finger board were seen by a few others as undignified. And since these particular others happened to include the board of trustees and conductor of the only symphony orchestra in the mountains of the North, Stretch's services in the orchestra had just been terminated. There weren't many other playing opportunities for a musician in his town, so he had a reason to be concerned.

But our hero was undaunted by even this frustration. "There must be a meaning hidden somewhere in this mess," he found himself thinking a few evenings later. Stretch really believed in his goodness as a human being. He also believed there was meaning in human existence. So he really tried to find some good, some growth, that could come from his misery.

Now it might seem odd that he didn't notice certain details in his life sooner, but then it's always easier to see things in other peoples' lives than it is to see them in our own. What's important is that Stretch finally came to ask the question, "What am I doing that's setting me up for all these problems?"

And then he finally realized. "Of course," he thought while he was enjoying one of his evening walks. "My whole life has been spent chasing whatever I felt would be most glamorous or most fun, without thinking at all about what I really ought to be doing. All this time I haven't thought once about my duty."

*This discovery brought him a deep sense of peace, and his little frame relaxed noticeably as he strolled quietly through that fine Autumn evening in the mountains of the North. Finally his mind bent toward the next question which probably would occur to most people who found themselves in such a situation. "But how," he asked, "am I supposed to **identify** my duty?"*

And then it hit him. Not any idea in particular. In fact, not an idea at all. What hit Stretch was a small bird. Steaming through the crisp evening air, it ran straight into the side of his head, tumbling coldly to the ground at his feet. This of course took him completely aback, as small missiles are apt to do when they run into your head when you least expect them. But Stretch regained his composure quickly, gently reaching down and picking up the little bird.

"How much you're like me," he whispered to his tiny cold friend, "racing through life without a thought to where you're really going."

Just then the tiny bird twitched, slowly opening one little eye to meet Stretch's concerned gaze.

"So you're alive!" he said quietly as he carefully placed his new friend onto a small patch of green moss nearby. "Let's see if you still can fly."

Immediately the little bird launched into a flurry of wing flapping. But sadly, just one wing flapped. The other simply hung outstretched at his side. Finally he collapsed in a ruffled heap at Stretch's feet.

Bending, Stretch turned toward home as he picked up the little bird once again. "Let's see if we can make a splint for your wing," he said as he walked briskly along. "I'll take care of you until you can fly again. That shouldn't be too hard to do."

On arriving home, it soon became clear that making a splint for such a tiny wing was by no means going to be easy. It wasn't that his little friend was uncooperative. Nothing could have been farther from the truth. Little Solomon, as he came to be called, barely moved as he watched Stretch fumble with hands much too large for the job that had to be done. Finally a crude splint was finished and bound gently to the tiny wing. And so began the process of healing for both of the little friends.

As time passed, Stretch and Solomon settled into an unusual, but sensible, routine. Solomon's needs were met easily and quickly in the morning, after which Stretch would relax a while, meditating on the new direction his life seemed to be taking. During this time Solomon would sit on the piano across from Stretch's chair, singing happily the way small birds frequently do just for the joy of it on the right kind of morning. Stretch found much of his best thinking going on during these moments. As he mused, he noticed that his life was changing rapidly. He had purchased woodworking tools shortly after Solomon's arrival. A peculiar feeling had overtaken him as he was working on the tiny bird's splint. He wasn't sure if the feeling sprang from compassion or from woodworking. But it was clear to him that while he was working on that splint he knew he was doing exactly what he should be doing. And he felt the deep sense of peace that comes when someone knows this.

"Maybe this is what I've been missing," he thought. "Maybe this is the way to tell if I've found my true duty." And of course he was quite right.

By Spring, Solomon's wing had healed enough to enable him to fly quite well, so Stretch released him as soon as the snow had melted. But Solomon never really left. Happily, the little bird returned regularly in the morning to sing just as he had sung on the piano. Stretch would move his chair outside when this happened, sitting and soaking in the warm inspiration of those moments.

As summer drifted into fullness, Stretch's woodworking gradually increased in purpose until he found himself beginning to make his first musical instrument. With help from several old books which were kindly lent from a distant library, he began cautiously to make his way through one of the turning points in his life. Within several months he finished his first opus, a faithful copy of his own string bass.

As it turned out this caused quite a stir, because the new instrument sounded every bit as good as his precious old one. At first this created a few problems as well, until his friends realized he really didn't want to part with his creation. "Why should I sell it?" he said. "I couldn't charge nearly what the sound is worth to me, since it doesn't have a famous name on it. And I really enjoy playing something I made myself."

And so Stretch's life gradually became quiet once again, but with an important difference. He finally felt respected by others. In fact, more than a few people from distant lands visited the little town in the mountains of the North just to see the new instrument maker and his wonderful string bass. Now this might all seem good enough, but fate was not quite finished dealing Stretch a winning hand.

As it turns out, the North Slope Symphony Orchestra had scheduled the world's finest string bass virtuoso to perform as soloist the following year. Time passed quickly for Stretch as he settled into his new feelings of self-esteem, working quietly to develop an improved bridge for his new instrument. By the time the big day arrived, our hero had become deeply absorbed in the work of the little shop that had sprung from his studio at home. He still sat regularly with Solomon, and he still took long walks, actually enjoying the crispness of the Autumn air. But his life had settled into an agreeable routine that was increasingly solitary, except for his little friend. For this reason he was surprised on that day to hear someone at his door. And he was even more surprised when he discovered who was knocking. He opened his door to find the most famous of all string bass players standing on his doorstep just shortly after arriving in town for the big performance.

"Dear sir," he began (Stretch had to try hard to keep from looking surprised at being addressed this way), "I have a problem that only you can solve. The bridge on my instrument is completely wrong for playing in the mountains of the North. I know you're skilled as an instrument maker, and I would be deeply appreciative if you could change the bridge before my performance this evening. I know this is an inconvenience, but I really am in a desperate situation and you're absolutely the only person I would trust with my instrument."

Now Stretch not only knew about this man's virtuosity as a performer, he also knew a great deal about the instrument the man regularly used. It was generally considered to be the finest string bass in the world, and it certainly was the most valuable.

"Of course," he replied in a slightly higher voice than usual. "I'd be honored. Come in and I'll start right away."

And so Stretch began immediately to work. As it turns out, he had finished his new style bridge, designed especially for the mountains of the North. Jonathon, the famous virtuoso, was very excited to see this as Stretch finished installing his handiwork. "What a fine idea," Jonathon said after trying his instrument. "I wonder why all bridges aren't made this way?"

"I don't know," Stretch replied. "I just made this because it works well here."

Then Jonathon asked, "Would it be possible for you to make another bridge of this style in the height I've been using in the city? I'd be happy to pay you whatever you'd want to charge."

By this time, Stretch was becoming quite excited. "Of course," he responded. "But instead of money, I'd really appreciate the chance to measure your wonderful instrument so I could try to make a reproduction of it for my own use. Would you mind?"

"Actually," Jonathon replied thoughtfully, "I'd be happy to let you do this, but I would like a favor in return. I'd like to be able to try the instrument when it's finished."

Now this really took Stretch by surprise. He was sure his voice shook a little as he replied "Of course."

Stretch quickly measured the famous string bass and promised to make a second bridge to match the original size before the evening. "I can deliver it to you after your performance this evening if you would like. I'll be there anyway."

"Wonderful," Jonathon replied as he jauntily turned to leave. "And I can't thank you enough for your help."

As it turned out, Jonathon had ample ways to thank Stretch. After finishing his solo, he turned to acknowledge Stretch in the audience. More than a few people had difficulty maintaining their composure when they saw the little man stand to accept the applause Jonathon so enthusiastically initiated.

After the performance, Stretch waited quietly near where Jonathon was accepting the congratulations of the conductor. Seeing him, Jonathon motioned for Stretch to join them. "Excuse me for just a moment," he said briskly as he turned to Stretch.

His voice warmed as he addressed Stretch, "You know I really wasn't looking forward to coming here. Most of my engagements are with the larger orchestras in the cities. But I've gotten more from this performance than from any in memory. Your work on my instrument has opened it up to nuances that were completely lost before. If there's anything I can do for you in return, contact me at any time.

I've written my private phone number for you. Please don't share it with anyone else, but really do call if you need or want anything. It really would be a pleasure to talk with you again when we both have time for more leisurely conversation. And please, do call me Jonathon."

Stretch tried to ignore the conductor's sweaty glare as he replied quietly, "Thanks Jonathon. I'll be in touch when the instrument is finished. Here's the other bridge. I put your old one with it. You've been really kind, and I appreciate that. Have a safe trip home."

The two friends shook hands briefly the way people do when they really mean it. Then Stretch turned and walked quietly from the concert hall. Jonathon's face became formal once again as he returned to his conversation with the conductor. Walking along, Stretch could hear hushed whispers, and he felt the hair stand up on the back of his neck as it does sometimes when people know they're being watched. At first he began to feel embarrassed, until he realized these were different from the derisive whispers he had heard so many times in the past. These were the muted sounds of respect and awe. Gradually he smiled as he walked from the hall, watching himself relax into a genuinely dignified stride.

Nearly a year passed before Stretch finished his reproduction of Jonathon's string bass. Fortunately Solomon had chosen not to migrate with the other birds that winter, preferring to remain indoors with Stretch in the North.

Stretch found the little bird's presence especially helpful whenever a feeling of urgency would overtake him. "Slow down," he would think as he sat listening to Solomon sing. "Nothing is more important than what you're doing right now."

Finally, when his work was complete, he was faithful to his promise. Within hours he called Jonathon in the city. As he dialed, he noticed his hand was trembling. Not much. Just a little, but enough to show he was a little anxious. Despite Jonathon's kindness and enthusiasm of a year before, Stretch wasn't at all certain what to expect.

His fears were put to rest immediately when Jonathon heard the news. "Wonderful!" he exclaimed. "How does it play?"

"As nearly as I can tell," Stretch replied, "it's the nicest string bass I've ever tried. But I've just played it for a few minutes, and I'm sure the post has to be moved."

After the slightest hesitation, he continued, "And you have to understand. I'm not used to playing instruments as fine as the ones you use. But I have to say, it's there for me more than I imagined any instrument could be. And the sound is a lot richer than I expected."

This launched a long and animated conversation culminating with Jonathon's promise to visit Stretch in his little shop as soon as he could.

Despite Jonathon's enthusiasm, Stretch was quite surprised to see him arrive the very next day. "I hope I'm not too soon," he said as Stretch invited him in, "but I was so excited I canceled my rehearsals for the next few days and booked the first available flight. Have you played it more?"

"I haven't stopped," Stretch replied through weary eyes. "And I haven't really slept. But I can't remember when I've had so much fun."

Passing the instrument to Jonathon, he piled into his sofa as he finished, "Here, it's your turn."

Jonathon ran his eyes carefully and quickly over the entire instrument. "It's beautiful," he said as he took his bow from its case.

Stretch closed his eyes as Jonathon's bow glided toward the strings. As he listened, it was impossible for him to tell exactly when the sound first began or where it was coming from. It just drifted into being with a smooth richness that seemed to flow from the air itself.

"That's a beautiful bow," Stretch said as he opened his eyes.

"I don't believe the bow is helping that much," Jonathon smiled. "I'm just letting the instrument do what it really wants."

Jonathon stayed on for several days, and when he finally did leave he took the new instrument with him. "I'll take good care of it, and I promise to return it within a month," he had promised. Of course Stretch was disappointed to see it leave so quickly even for just a while, but he knew that Jonathon would care for it well. And he knew he'd be able to play it better than ever when it returned, because of the techniques Jonathon had shared while they tested the instrument.

Except for the moments outside with Solomon, time passed slowly for the next few weeks. His little friend of course helped him a great deal. It wasn't that Stretch worried about Jonathon. He just missed his new string bass. But this was enough to settle him into a kind of tingling flatness that people sometimes mistake for depression. The kind of feeling that sometimes opens a person to deep peace.

Occasionally when this happened, Solomon would find a special song that would open Stretch to the spaciousness that can come from such a feeling. He found his mind became crystal clear as he sat in that state. So it was natural that when his mind bent then to duty, he understood it a little better than he had before.

As he sat during one of those special moments, he thought, "I didn't realize how self involved I was while I was making the new bass. It's so nice to have this time to settle down again. This is what I'm really supposed to do. Nothing is more important than sitting here right now." And so he sat, free at last from his desire to be in the spotlight, peaceful in the solitude of the moment.

Stretch's faith in Jonathon was not misplaced. True to his word Jonathon appeared before the end of the month to return the instrument. As he arrived, he passed a folder of papers to Stretch.

"I thought you might enjoy these," he said as he settled onto the sofa.

Stretch quickly opened the folder to find over a dozen newspaper reviews.

"Those are the reviews of my performances since I borrowed your new instrument," Jonathon said cheerfully. "I've highlighted the parts you'll probably enjoy the most."

Stretch's eyes widened as he read the first review. "You used my bass!" he exclaimed.

"Of course," came the reply. "Why not? It's as good as anything I own, and it seems to be getting better by the day."

"You know," Jonathon continued, "I don't need another instrument, but if you ever decide to part with this one I'd really appreciate a chance to buy it. I promise I won't bother you for it, but please give me a chance if the time ever comes. In the meantime, I'd like to hear you play it with this."

As he spoke, Jonathon removed a beautiful old bow from its case and handed it to Stretch. "This is for you. It seems to like your instrument better than it likes mine."

It took Stretch a while to learn how to accommodate his new instrument, but with his new bow and Jonathon's help he soon was comfortable just drawing the tone from the instrument, instead of driving at it the way he had done before. And what a tone it was. As he was leaving for home, Jonathon said quietly, "You know, you could please anyone anywhere playing the way you do now. You might consider giving a recital in the city, if you'd have time to work one up."

By this time Jonathon knew Stretch pretty well, but perhaps not quite so well as he had thought. So he was a little surprised when Stretch hesitated before replying, "That sounds wonderful, but I'll have to run it by Solomon. I'll call you in a week or two if it seems like a good idea. Either way I really appreciate your kindness. I understand what you're offering to do for me."

Jonathon gave Stretch one of those "I don't understand but it doesn't matter" looks that friends sometimes give friends, then smiled and left for home. Stretch immediately took his favorite chair outside and sat waiting for Solomon to appear.

Before long the little bird flew into view and flitted down next to his friend.

"Thanks for coming," Stretch began. "I just don't know what to do. Just when I'm secure in my happiness here, sure that I'm doing my duty, I'm given a chance to do what I've always wanted. It seemed so right for me to be in the background. Now I'm given this opportunity the same way I was given my peaceful duty in my shop. It seems like it would be wrong for me to

refuse, but I just can't bear to leave the peace and contentment I've finally found here."

This caused Stretch to pause suddenly. "That's it!" he said excitedly. "If I identify my duty by the feeling of peace it gives me, then what Jonathon is offering me is wrong. I don't want to go back to the turmoil of performing."

And then he paused again, this time slumping a little as he continued in a weary voice. "But I guess my duty isn't to do just what I want to do. And I can't see what I really want now anyway, much less where my duty lies. I feel lazy when I don't want to do the recital, and I feel agitated when I think how nice it would be to perform in the city. How can my duty lie in either direction? But these are my only choices. My peace here has been destroyed, and I have nowhere to turn. Why would I be given all of this only to have it taken away? It's just not fair." So saying, he settled resolutely into his chair as Solomon began to sing.

Immediately he heard his inner voice. Although later he would say he had heard words, he never would be able to recall them. But he never would forget the moment when he realized the nature of duty. In one quiet flash he saw what had eluded him for so long. He realized his duty wasn't concerned with performing or with making instruments. But he saw why it was so right for him to have spent time in his shop. He saw, in other words, that duty isn't really concerned with what we're doing so much as how we do it. And he knew that the time spent in his shop had opened him to doing things the right way. Finally it all made sense. He had been right in thinking that duty is identified correctly by a feeling of peace. But he had mistaken duty for what was done, rather than how it was done. He saw that even his woodworking could have been done egoistically. And he saw that this would not have brought him peace and happiness, regardless of how well his instruments might have turned out.

Gradually regaining his presence, Stretch watched Solomon for a while. He thanked his friend through shining eyes, then rose to his work.

Stretch did prepare a recital, which was received quite well. But he didn't linger long in the city. Instead, he returned to his little town in the mountains of the North. Within a few months, he had accepted a position in the string bass section of the North Slope Symphony, refusing their offer of the principal chair. "What's wrong with the fine young man who has been principal for several years?" he had asked. "He did well enough to please you last year, and I expect he'll do the same again. I'll be quite happy just being on stage surrounded by the sound of the orchestra."

Stretch lives on in the little town in the mountains of the North. More than a few envy his small size, which they take to be part of the secret of his amazing longevity. But what's important, he uses his time well, growing in wisdom as the years pass. This is why people come from near and far seeking his company and counsel.

With so many people coming by, it's inevitable that a few will challenge him with questions such as, "But what if I'm moved to do something really bad? Suppose I want to kill someone? Is this my duty?"

When this happens, Stretch takes a deep breath then looks to see if the person is earnest. If so, he's likely to reply, "Only if it's given. If we desire something egoistically, then it's not our duty no matter what it is. Even killing can be right or wrong. Killing a murderer who is about to murder again might be a good thing. But the goodness wouldn't spring from the external circumstances alone. Killing even in those circumstances would be bad, if we did it in anger. But if we did it in sorrow for the taking of a life, and in a spirit of humility and compassion, the quality of our act would be good. Goodness and duty are determined by the inside of an act. The outside of any act is merely the product of the inside. Our motives determine the quality of what we do - the real issue is where we're coming from. When we surrender our pride we cannot make a wrong choice. An enthusiastic and uninvolved action simply can't be wrong."

Mel felt her voice change, realizing how distant it had been. Turning to Yew, she spoke softly, "I think I understand what this means, but why is duty so important?"

Yew smiled, "You know from Young that we have to recognize ego in order to trust our judgment. Understanding duty helps with this. Competence and duty never actually occur alone. We can talk about them in isolation, but we always actually find them together. When duty becomes completely clear, we find compassion and competence, fearlessness and happiness... and freedom from ego.

Society benefits when we find duty this well because it means we've opened ourselves to compassion and competence. We benefit directly as well. Compassion opens us to real happiness, and complete competence rides on freedom from ego, which frees us from fear. We benefit, and society benefits, in all these ways when we realize our duty. And we move toward enlightenment."

Mel's eyes brightened and she began talking more quickly, "I think I finally get it."

Yew smiled gently as he replied, "Yes, but it's a deep dream, and thoughts emerging from depth have richness that isn't always immediately obvious. Tell me what you see."

Mel breathed a long slow breath, waiting for the Chi that would help her center. When she felt it she began, "At first I thought the dream was telling me to make sure I was doing the right thing, that my feeling of peace would show me I was doing my duty. But toward the end of the dream I realized that duty doesn't emerge as a job, it emerges as a way of doing. It emerges *through* a way of doing. I don't believe peace and happiness come from getting or doing anything in particular. I believe they come as a by-product of doing something well. And I finally realize what this means. For a long time I've felt that doing something well meant doing it proficiently. Now I realize it refers to origin, not product. But this seems wrong somehow. Doesn't duty have anything to do with the quality of its product?"

"Of course it does," Yew said. "When I'm moved properly to act, my actions fit my disposition, and this helps. Now I may want to change my disposition, but that change begins when I get out of the way, when I pause to respond without my ego whenever I'm about to act. Eventually this becomes automatic, and I find my disposition actually has changed. And when this occurs, I find my duty has changed as well. But even at the beginning of this transformation my proficiency is enhanced, because I'm working earnestly, but not feverishly."

Mel felt Yew's gaze. She knew he felt her confusion as he continued, "If you think about it, we function better this way because even though we want as much as ever to do things well we have less and less to lose. As a result, competency improves as our motives are transformed. We have less to lose, since we're shedding the ego involvement in our work. Ego after all is all we stand to lose or gain ultimately from our actions. Then as our ego involvement continues to wane, our proficiency becomes even more enhanced by our increased detachment. Enthusiasm continues to grow, which helps as well. In the end, we're just the vehicle, not the driver. We work hard to prepare the best possible vehicle, then we give control of the vehicle to a more competent hand."

Mel felt her enthusiasm growing as she joined in, "Then Stretch really was creating an instrument within himself even more than he was creating an instrument that the world could see. And when his inner instrument was finished he was able to perform as an instrument rather than as the performer, so his peace and happiness were enhanced while he did the same job that had made him miserable before."

"Yes," Yew responded. "And this would have been true whether or not his status had changed, although it's hard to imagine how such a transformation could occur without affecting others."

"You know," Yew continued after a pause, "Peace is hard to see in the midst of the battle we're sometimes called to by duty, but it can be found, so long as duty is done for its sake alone.

All we have to do is look with our heart instead of just our intellect. After all, intellect is only the outer surface of our awareness. That's the domain of ego, and we need to be free from its blindness.

It's foolish to look for peace of mind through others who are tied to their own needs and expectations. All we have to do is listen to the silence. Peace comes to any heart that has opened to the truth of duty, and this can be found in the silence. When we accept the wisdom of silence we can live and die in peace and happiness."

Smiling, he continued. "It's not easy to see duty. How can we distinguish duty from something less innocent that might seem the same? We have to purify ego for this. Ego builds an instrument of quality in a focused mind. But then it has to realize that its ability is in preparing the instrument, not in performing with it. For true greatness, the real creative artist must be released to perform, must be given the finely tuned instrument of the mind to play in this world. *Duty lives in purification of mind and ego, and in acceptance of what is given.*"

Mel knew from his pause that Yew was finished. Her heart pounded, sensing this was her last chance to ask whatever she wanted to ask. Groping for some way to get him to continue, she fell into her next words, "Then the true greatness that was Stretch's destiny was an inner thing."

"Yes," Yew grinned. "Stretch found he was destined for true greatness, but only when he allowed greatness to find him instead of seeking it directly. It had to find him as a result of his innocent response to duty. He couldn't have found it by seeking it directly, egoistically. True greatness, after all, doesn't come merely from doing something well."

Harley, who had been sitting silently all this time, leaned forward a bit as he asked, "But how about all the great artists who are so self-involved?"

Yew faced Harley as he replied, "True greatness isn't measured by career or fame. It's a different sort of thing. It's not a result of external skill the way it might seem. It's merely a natural product of proper response to duty."

Harley's desperate look pushed Yew to continue. "Look into anyone who is self-involved," he said gently, "and you'll find a knot of frustration and fear. Whenever we're self-involved we can feel this knot to some extent within ourselves if we look honestly. Ego involvement tightens the knot.

True greatness has no need for this. It doesn't matter how successful or how great someone might seem to others. If they're self-involved they'll have a nagging feeling that somehow they're not as successful or as appreciated as they ought to be. And they'll be driven by a hardness within their heart in spite of themselves."

Yew smiled, "Ego seems to be good, because it gives us a feeling of entitlement. But ego can't get rid of the knot. We discover this whenever we strive to be free. We think we're trying to let go, but we're really hanging on to the very thing that makes us miserable. When we let go of ego, we see that the knot has disappeared. As long as we depend on ego for our motivation and resolve, we cling to the miserable knot. This is okay if we need to get moving, but sooner or later we have to come to peace. Then we have to turn to duty instead of pride, because duty releases us to self-mastery. This is a happy, a peaceful, state. This is true freedom."

Mel fidgeted. She knew she had another question, but she just couldn't remember it. Finally it came.

"Go ahead," Yew said as her face lit up.

"Thanks. I've been trying to come to grips with the idea of reincarnation ever since you talked about it. It was just beginning to feel natural when I made the mistake of talking with an atheist friend. Now I'm back to the beginning again. I know you believe it's true. But why? It seems like such an assumption."

"Your atheist friend must be pretty smart to set you back like that. Atheism can be pretty convincing when it's presented in a rational way. But it loses its strength when we look at it closely, because then we see it's not really rational at all.

Let's take a look at what atheism says. In religious terms, it asserts that the universe cannot possibly spring from a ground of pure goodness. Experience demonstrates this. In this picture, the idea of reincarnation seems pretty silly, since there's no reason to believe in the existence of a prerequisite ground. Actually, rational atheistic belief is a negative faith in the nonexistence of God. It must be a faith, because the atheist accepts only rational proof and atheism cannot be proven rationally to be true. Beyond this, atheism asserts that God cannot exist, and this requires a denial of any experience suggesting that the existence of order is rooted in good.

In the end, atheism is a negative mirror of a shallow faith in the existence of God. Both are built on an incomplete evaluation of experience. Both make concrete assertions based on incomplete experience.

Both assume a low level of potential for human experience. Shallow religious faith assumes this because fear of death pushes us to accept authoritative word about the limits of experience as a condition for salvation. Shallow atheistic faith is pushed by fear too. The atheist's pride won't admit error, so it is easy to assert without proof that legitimate human knowledge is limited by rationality, ignoring the truth of scientific method.

When we live in our intelligence, it's hard to see how our thinking is shaped by pride. I might feel, for instance, that I'm a completely rational being, clear thinking and free from the fear that pushes people into shallow faith. Once this kind of play is started, it takes on a life of its own. Proud of my Clarity, I assume that my incomplete rational experience is as complete as anyone's experience is ever going to get. And since my rational experience doesn't recognize God, God cannot exist.

I assume from pride what those of shallow faith in God assume from fear of death. That is, I assume human experience is necessarily limited so we can never know certain things. I see that my thinking isn't clouded by a fear of death, but I don't see the pride that pushes me to mistake partial experience for complete proof. I don't see my pride, so I can't see my fear pushing me to accept partial experience of truth as conclusive proof to preserve my feeling of being right. I can clearly see the evils and flux that are essential to the universe, but since I don't happen to see the emergence of the universe from a dynamic of good, I assume no such dynamic can possibly exist. And I categorically refuse to accept rationally coherent explanations, like reincarnation, that don't fit with my limited experience and background."

Yew paused, seeing the vacant look in Mel's eyes.

When she relaxed, he continued, "Fortunately, there's another possibility too. Everyone's experience can include the emergence of Clarity, peace, and compassion. Without fail, these wonders come to fill the space made whenever we relax enough to loosen the grip of our ego. This is the way it goes with everyone who relaxes completely. Seeing this in others who similarly relax corroborates the truth of our beliefs. It shows that the ground of our individual selves is good. We can see that God is not coercive because we have freedom to do as we wish. But our essence in truth is neither chaotic nor evil.

When experience is rich enough to see this, debating philosophy isn't so important any more. Then the issue changes. Why should we care if reincarnation exists? Fear has surrendered to freedom, and the issue of reincarnation is largely an issue because of rational fear. The issue lingers, but in a new way. We still need a picture of the universe that is inclusive of all experience, and since the atheistic picture denies a ground of goodness, it no longer makes sense. With enough experience, the idea of reincarnation is just another part of a coherent picture of existence. So even though it doesn't matter in the same way, it still matters.

With our heart bending more and more toward purification, clear and rational belief takes on new importance. More than ever we want to shelter ourselves from wasted time and life energy, so we need a clear view of the way things really are. This kind of belief turns us away from fear, away from clinging to the source of our misery, and helps us avoid wasted time and energy.

Cultivating this isn't easy. Pride is subtle, and so long as it has our ear we continue to believe we're being open-minded when we're not. Pride can make us blind to the flinch that pushes us from rational options that are unattractive simply because they don't fit with what we call our own.

If we don't see our pride, we won't see the flinch that undermines our rationality and we won't notice the anger that should alert us to our intractability. So we continue clinging to the source of our misery, blind to our misuse of intellect as we confuse tenacity with rigor. But there is hope. Over time this happens less and less until we are free.

Pride, after all, isn't completely bad. When misery builds until we can't ignore it any longer, pride can give us courage to turn toward peace instead. When relief becomes more important than the pride we feel in our rationality, courage can help us take our first step toward freedom. Just learning to relax is enough. The rest will follow, but we're still vulnerable. Clarity comes to an open mind, but pride can conceal itself well even in our experience of relaxing and healing.

If we keep our eye on relief rather than success, and if we let ourselves be drawn to experiences of quiet rather than activity regardless of how attractive the activity might seem, then our experience will tend to shelter us from pride. Protection is important too, but shelter is essential and it is an issue of purification, not power. Everything comes naturally when we become purified. Look outwardly for the source of your problems and they will never end. Look inwardly, and the whole world will be your own. Remember, your real issue is purification."

He finished and they sat in silence for a while. When it was clear that there would be no more questions, he said, "Before I go I should tell you a few things about Marjorie. I've been her friend for many years, and am indebted to her in the same way that you are indebted to me. I'm here because she wanted me to bring you along until you were ready to move on. That time has come."

Mel tried to speak, but couldn't.

Yew continued, "I'm sure you have many questions about her, so I will tell you what I can. I met Marjorie many years ago while wandering the mountains of Asia. I was seeking a teacher who I could trust with my life.

It was late in the day, and I was thankful to find a small cave that led into the mountain from a ledge above the Ganges. In the mountains the Ganges River is a torrent of melting ice, so its sound filled the air as I made my way in. I soon found that the cave was much larger than it appeared from the outside, and it was occupied.

145

I knew at once that I had stumbled into a sanctified space. The roar of the river produced a constant sound of "OM" that seemed to intensify as I went deeper into the mountainside. After a while, my eyes began to adjust to the darkness and I could make out a light some distance ahead. Making my way carefully, I eventually reached the end of the tunnel, where a single candle burned on a small altar. In front of the altar sat a small man.

I was very uncomfortable. I had entered a holy spot without permission and interrupted a holy man's meditation, but I couldn't leave. The atmosphere of the cave and the feeling of warmth and peace that came from the silent man were too strong. So I forgot myself and just sat quietly behind him. I was mortified when the voice of a woman finally asked, "What is it you wish?"

This destroyed what was left of my composure. I spoke as best I could. "Please excuse me for disturbing you, good Mother. I meant no offense. I thought you were a man. I never would have come into your dwelling place had I known otherwise."

"What is the difference, if your aim is spiritual?"

What happened next was odd. Her voice had such a calming effect that all my fear left me. As soon as I found my tongue I was filled with questions. Who was she? How long had she been in the cave? Was she a yogini? She listened without a word. When I had finished completely, she finally spoke. Her name was Marjorie. She was English. And she had been in the cave nearly 15 years. As to the rest, she was very vague. She seemed to take an interest in my comfort, but beyond that she didn't seem to care at all what I was thinking.

I was ecstatic. I thought that I might have found the teacher I had been looking for. So I began asking more pointed questions. I was determined to know if I finally had found a realized soul.

"Have you experienced all that is to be experienced?"

"I can't say if there is more, but I have been given enough."

At that moment I knew I had found who I was looking for, but a big question still was unanswered. Not all illumined souls are teachers. Many live their lives in solitude, and there were no signs that other people frequented the cave. I knew I had to be very delicate now with my questions.

"If you are English, you may have experience with a problem I have been having. How do you respond to people who say you are damned because you do not share their religious convictions?"

"God touches me directly many times each day. I can't worry about the negative opinions of someone who has never been touched in this way."

"But some of them are religious figures, and they can be extremely aggressive. It's hard to ignore what they say, especially when it is extremely disquieting."

"Aggressiveness is a mark of fear. Fear is a mark of ignorance. This is a telling sign in one who is giving spiritual advice."

"How is fear a mark of ignorance?"

"When we discover the true nature of things, we realize there is nothing to fear. We don't need to defend our views because we are not afraid they are wrong. We share when it is appropriate and we feel the suffering of others who are afraid. But we have no desire to attack them, because they have nothing we need."

"Does this mean that anyone who is aggressive against me is attacking me because I have something they need? This doesn't always seem to be the case. What would an evangelist hope to gain from their aggressiveness with me?"

"Salvation, perhaps. Some are taught that they will suffer if they don't convert others by any means necessary. And too, they may simply need to have their fears calmed by forcing someone else to admit that they are right. After all, a lot seems to be at stake. And some might just be after the feeling of power or social elevation they get by manipulating others. They might believe they are being noble when they really are just being controlling."

"Then is there any sign that I can use to tell when I should listen?"

"Yes. God's word invariably is marked with quiet and compassion. It may be hard to see, because truth is not necessarily what we expect or want to hear. But if we are alert to our own activity we will see the mark of God if it is there."

"Does this mean that God is separate, a thing that leaves a mark?"

"Not for me. The God of my experience is indistinguishable from the Self that does the seeing. But there is no doubt that the God of my experience could manifest in form as well."

Then I asked my question, "Do you accept students?"

"I have no students. But I do have a few wonderful friends, and I would be happy if you wished to be one of them."

Yew continued, "As it turns out, I spent a long while in Marjorie's company. After some time in the mountains I assisted her with her travels. Each year we visited her friends in various parts of the world. Eventually she settled in the little home where you now live. At the time, I knew she was waiting for someone. She still waits, but the time is near for you to meet again."

No one said a word as Yew rose quietly and moved toward the door. He turned and said, "Thank you. Both of you are wonderful friends." Then he was gone.

Mel felt her chest sag as she watched Yew disappear. She knew she would never see him again. Even though she felt in her heart of hearts that this didn't matter, that he had given her what she really needed, she felt alone for the first time since they had met.

"So this is what depression feels like," she brooded darkly, slumping into the wall.

After a while of this she lifted her eyes to find Harley quietly watching. As their eyes met, Mel felt a warm surge of energy, the same energy she had felt from Yew, filling her. And she saw Harley was weeping.

"Oh my God," she cried to herself, "He's weeping for me. He's not even aware of what's happening. He has such power. Yew's power must have come through compassion too."

As she continued watching, Harley seemed to change. Soon his weeping was gone and he was absolutely motionless. Even his breathing seemed to disappear as his eyes gazed unwaveringly into the distance. And she noticed he seemed to be glowing. Not much, but enough so Mel was sure she wasn't mistaken.

Mel felt a tear roll down her cheek as she surrendered to the moment.

The next thing Mel knew she was opening her eyes to find sunlight streaming through the closet window. She felt refreshed even though she obviously had spent the night sitting on her pillow. But above all she felt very happy, not at all the way she had anticipated in her darker musings about the possibility of Yew's departure.

Looking around, she saw Harley once again watching her quietly. As their eyes met they both stood and moved quietly toward their own New World.

***

The day passed quickly, as busy days frequently do. Mel reached her computer by 8:00 AM. An hour later the entire Project staff was assembled in the Gallery. No one knew why they were there, but Mel's message had been emphatic.

MANDATORY MEETING IN GALLERY AT 9:00 AM SHARP

CLOSE ALL OFFICES

Mel talked softly into the silence. "The Project has reached another turning point. As of tomorrow, Jason Alteridge will be Senior Project Administrator. Both Harley and I will continue helping as we can, but it is time for the project to move on. We need to begin right now to convert all the Project labs into meditation rooms. We've constructed a model in Research III with the help of Yew, the evening custodian. We'll be happy to help others duplicate it."

Before the whispering could start, Mel continued, "You should all know that the first stage of our research has been completed. With the help of Yew, we have found a way to heal the disease. Once the rooms are converted we need to move toward the second stage and begin to help others. Yew has shown us how to do this too."

"There's no way to stop the whispering now," Mel said quietly to Harley as she took a long sip of her water.

When things had become relatively calm, Mel continued, "Everybody has job security as long as they want it, but a lot of duties have to change. The purpose of the project is to discover healing, and then to share it. We can't safely help others until we've become unburdened ourselves. The sooner we get started, the sooner this will happen."

By the end of the day, computers were packed and carpets ordered. Although she was extremely weary, Mel felt effortlessly alert. This changed when she reached home. Walking straight to her bed, she was asleep almost as soon as her head touched her pillow.

Chapter 12

Truth in Passing

Waking slowly, Mel reached for the only note she had ever gotten from Yew. It had arrived the day after his departure, and she read it often.

Dear Mel,

This prayer was a gift of sleep. Although given to me, I felt it might speak to you as well.

When the burdens of time start to cover my view
Of life's beauty and purpose and even of You
As You work ever gently to soften my heart,
Making way with Your love for another fresh start;
As I strain to pursue what seems right to my mind,
Never heeding the voice that says "leave it behind";
Let me see with my heart, without need for my eyes.

Let me use this fresh start to begin now to rise
From within all the hardness which seems to arrive
To consume all my efforts whenever I strive
With my mind and my actions to show that I can
Merely act in the interests of my fellow man.
Let me now, just this once, listen just with my heart.

Let my actions be Your actions, flowing to start

My release from the bonds which alone I have made,

And which bind me most tight when I wish them to fade.

Let me see that my struggles are struggles with pride.

Let me see with my heart what is waiting inside.

You never have to feel alone. Marjorie will return soon, and you are with me always.

Love,

Yew

Sliding from her bed, Mel folded the note and carefully returned it to its envelope. Sooner or later, the letter would have to be shared.

Private time was easier to find now, but she began her day before most of the others. The stars were still shining as she reached the closet. Mel smiled to see Harley on his pillow as she slid into place.

By dawn they were pouring tea. The closet had been connected to the room next door, which served as a lounge. "We simply shouldn't eat in the closet," she had told Jason. She expected an argument.

Instead, he smiled and replied softly, "Fine. Let's see if we can set up the room next door for you and Harley. There's no point in saving a few dollars if it gets in the way of the only thing that's important."

Mel wondered occasionally at the change in Jason. He had fallen into his new responsibilities much more gracefully than anyone had anticipated.

"Don't worry," Mel had said. "He has what he wants. Now that he's on top, he has everything to gain and nothing to lose by helping us succeed."

But underneath it all everyone did worry, especially Mel. She had no way to know that he had received a letter too.

Jason looked at the envelope. There was no return address. "It figures," he mumbled. "The first piece of mail in my new office and I can't even tell who it came from. I hope they bothered to sign it."

Sliding through the door, he settled into the oversized chair behind his desk. But he didn't move right away to the letter. It couldn't be that important, if they hadn't even bothered to put their name on it. There was time to savor the rich wood walls of his new environment. After a few minutes of this, Jason realized he wasn't really seeing the walls, so he turned to the letter. Opening it briskly, he began to read.

Dear Jason,

I expect that right now you are very happy with your success. It's good your desire has been satisfied. Now you can move on.

You stand at a critical juncture. If you wish, it's easy to spend the rest of your life protecting what you've finally gotten, unable to enjoy what you felt you wanted all those years. Or you can choose a new direction, moving toward what you really want.

The thrill of this moment will pass quickly, so you must act now. Opportunities to see between moments are rare. Look now, before you're swept away by a new desire, and things will be clear.

Look to your happiness. Find its measure. What in your life has left you with a feeling of happiness? What moments are warmest in your recollection? What experiences made you live in the present moment? Find the thread running through your happiness and don't let distractions pull you away. Know what you really want, and it will be yours.

There was no signature.

Jason looked at the walls once again. The wood looked rich and beautiful. "Why didn't it look like this a moment ago?" he thought aloud. As he wondered, his mind drifted across his life. The memory of the day he bought his first new car felt barren. Turning from this, he thought about the day he bought his house. "These aren't the moments that made me happy," he realized. "It's the same as looking at the walls before I read the letter. Even though I had gotten what I wanted, I wasn't really enjoying it. Something was missing."

Finally his mind arrived on the day Mel told him she was moving from her office, giving it to him. "Something was there," he said to himself. "But it was gone when I finally moved in. What made it come back?"

Looking again at the letter, he realized. "Warmth. I wasn't expecting it, but that moment gave me one of the warmest feelings of my life. Just like the feeling I had now looking at the wood. That must be a key to the real happiness in my life. But where does it come from? What other experiences have felt this way?"

It didn't take long for Jason to recall many moments of warmth, and seeing them, he saw the thread. "That's it," he thought. "It doesn't matter how little or large a gift is. It just matters if it flows from compassion. Mel felt real compassion for me when she gave me this room. It was part of the gift, even if I didn't see it. All my happy memories are filled with love. There's no connection between the stuff I got and how happy it made me. Happiness comes from being near compassion."

Jason looked again at the wall, and he knew the rest. "Of course. I'm not enjoying the wood or anything else when I'm driven. I have to live more quietly. I have to learn to let down if I'm going to allow compassion to be part of my life. I guess I don't have any choice. I don't want to be miserable any more."

The project couldn't have been in better hands.

Chapter 13

Coming Around

Mel enjoyed spending time in her favorite chair on the porch. Spring was beginning to color the woods, so the view was especially beautiful and the air was becoming warm. Although only a few weeks had passed since handing over her responsibilities to Jason, she was completely accustomed to having more private time. She was pleased to see herself settling into a routine that used her new time wisely. She continued practicing in the closet, but had much more time for reading and meditating at home.

She did have other responsibilities. Each morning she and Harley went to the Gallery for meditation with the entire staff. After meditating they talked a while with the group. This was followed frequently by an hour or two of private conversations, but the rest of the day was their own. Jason had arranged things carefully. He knew that she and Harley could finish their morning practice in the closet comfortably before the staff gathering, and he made certain that everyone respected the two's need for privacy later in the day.

Typically Mel and Harley would eat lunch together in his apartment, then go their separate ways until evening. With no particular plan, he usually arrived at her home around suppertime, lingering a while after. He always returned to his own place for the night. It was not a typical romantic relationship, but Mel found it deeply satisfying. It seemed odd for Harley to be the only real uneasiness in her life. Their relationship was very close, and very comfortable in every way but one. Yew was gone, and she had heard nothing from

Marjorie. What was she supposed to do? It would have been perfectly natural for Harley to move into the little house with her, but she couldn't bring herself to do that without Marjorie's permission. She smiled when she thought how this would look to a therapist. Here she was, the shining example of freedom and self-sufficiency for so many others, and she was completely dependent on someone else's approval for her biggest decisions.

Mel laughed as she thought about her incredible good fortune. It all seemed so ordinary until she stepped back and looked. As natural as things were, she laughed each time she put it into words. She knew she was just beginning her path, but it was wonderful to be free from the fear and pain that had been such a part of life. Although her path still stretched beyond sight, she felt for the first time that it really didn't matter.

"There's nothing to fear in returning. The gifts I have now will be waiting to be discovered again. And it doesn't matter if I'm not finished when I die. I'll be back anyway. I just can't turn away from the suffering."

Mel enjoyed the change in seasons. She was happy to bring her big pillow back to it's summer spot. It had a companion now. Both were placed carefully on the rear of the porch floor where they would be sheltered from the weather. She had not sat on Marjorie's pillow since that first day, wrapping it carefully and putting it in a linen closet almost immediately. Replacing it with another she had found inside, she had used the new one frequently for meditating on the porch. It was low enough for privacy, but she still could see the woods as she sat. She did this quite often. Between the chair and the pillow, she spent hours on the porch each day.

The air was damp, so she went inside to fix a pot of tea. Returning to her chair with a steaming cup, she sat looking into the woods. As always, she was overtaken by the feelings that were a part of this place. She had been sitting for a while when a movement caught her eye. Someone was coming down the trail. There was something familiar about the way they walked. Then she knew. It was Yew's walk, quick and graceful at the same time. Pausing in the shade, he looked for a long while at the porch. Seeing her, he stepped into the clearing and Mel realized she was mistaken. It wasn't Yew; it was his teacher. Mel stood as Marjorie walked lightly to the porch.

"Your chair is warm and waiting. Would you like something to drink? I've just finished making some herb tea I think you'll enjoy."

About the Author

David McGuire has degrees in Music, Religion, and Philosophy, and has finished the coursework for a Ph.D. in Philosophy at Pennsylvania State University.

Currently teaching music at Cleveland State University and The College of Wooster, David also performs as oboist with the Cleveland Opera and the Cleveland Chamber Symphony. Originally trained as a symphony orchestra musician, he retired from full time performing in 1970. At that time his career was curtailed by lung problems that brought unanticipated spiritual opportunity through the Grace of a Raja Yoga Master who intervened to restore David to health as he was dying at the Cleveland Clinic Hospital.

Performing only part time since then, David has been free to devote his time to a personal practice of Yoga along with an ongoing search for ways to integrate Eastern truths and methods into a Western lifestyle. In addition to teaching meditation techniques as part of a university curriculum, he has taught yoga informally in the United States and Canada. His ongoing practice recently included studying Reiki with Michael and Donna Goode in Lindsay, Ontario. David was certified in Canada as a Reiki Master in 1999.

Printed in the United States
2707